WHEN SHE WRITES

POEMS AND SHORT STORIES
BY RACHAEL HINKLEY

Copyright 2025 Rachael Hinkley

All rights reserved. No part of this book may be reproduced, stored in a retrieval system or transmitted in any form, or by any means, without the prior written permission of the author or publisher except by a reviewer who may quote brief passages to be printed in a newspaper, magazine or journal.

Cover Art by Rachael Hinkley. Photography by Rachael Hinkley. Graphic Art by Rachael Hinkley. All rights reserved.

First Edition

First Printing

Published by Rachael Hinkley

Inspiration

"Fear freezes your ability to push forward. Courage and discipline breaks the ice and thaws out the notion of "I'm afraid , therefore, I can't."

-Rae Hinkley

Dedication

There is not one single individual I can attribute this version of my creativeness to. I owe it all to the creator.

The Calling in the Cold

It never really gets cold in South Carolina, not even in the most dreadful of winters. Something about the crisp coolness of those winter nights however, does make you welcome a hot cup of something and a blanket while you curl up in an oversized chair and contemplate life. The days are tolerable and have you wondering how those in the north endure their long arduous winters. The notion sends a shiver to my core and I pull my cardigan closer around me and thank the gods I am in a state of tolerable cold and moderate dreary. Not as depressing and easier on my fragile mental state. A refreshing and excellent decision to be closer to something I love.

Taking my now empty coffee cup into the kitchen for a refill, I stop at the sink and watch the night dance out of the window above. I reach to open it just a tad, so I can smell the cool salty air of the ocean that lies fifty feet from it. The salt water fills my lungs and I am reminded of why I came here to begin with. I am reminded of the darkness I left behind. I can still hear the screams in the night from the terror and stress of the life

I left. I inhale deeply, letting the salty goodness clear my mind in preparation of what I must do again. Wondering why I decided to even entertain what waits for me in a brown cardboard evidence box on my table.

I told myself when I moved here I would not ever get involved in things that would haunt my sleep, that I wanted a more simple life, one I could ride the rest of my years out in moderate peace. I had a few years of that very thing, a few peaceful, restful, years. At least I got that, a taste of it anyways. A tantalizing, addictive, fucking taste. I inhaled again and closed my eyes, and let the sweet surrender of the oceanic air prepare me to even open the box on my table. The one that has sat untouched since I brought it home from my office a week ago.

I wasn't prepared for even the consideration. I left that life behind. Settled on a quiet life on the beach, one I could live out the rest of my days not adding more scars. Short lived by the phone call I hesitated to answer, knowing damn well he wasn't calling to catch up.

" I told you Sam, I am retired. How did you even get this number?"

"Johnnie, I know, I know ,and I am truly sorry, do you know how hard it has been for me to not call you? I have had this case for three months just sitting strewn everywhere on my desk."

" Ok and, I am not interested, I told you.."

" Johnnie, Johanna… Please, just look at it, that's all I am asking."

That was not all he was asking and I knew it. I knew and I told him to send it anyway. When will I ever get away from his hold on me I will never know. The box came three days later via messenger , which told me it was already in route during that phone call. Damn him to hell for knowing me. Damn him.

The box was not very heavy, the label on it stated that it was a Jane Doe case. I closed my eyes and took a deep breath, running my hand over the lid, nudging it slightly up only to slam it back and curse Sam once more. I walked over to the window in my office and pushed it open and lit a cigarette. Smoking was not an easy habit to kick. I took a long drag on it and let the embers burn bright in my eyes. Staring out of the window I was transported back to my last Jane Doe case, the one that led me to retirement and to this quiet little neck of the woods working for a small town tax attorney. Not much bloody gore in investigating tax fraud.

Finishing the cigarette, I put it out in the ashtray that sat on the window sill and closed the window.

I caught a glimpse of my reflection in the window and saw the exhaustion and darkness slowly creep in. I knew I would help and I knew I could solve it, what I didn't know is where this darkness would leave me once it was over. I took the box and its mysterious contents to my house where it has sat on my table ever since.

Setting my coffee cup on the table, I scooted my chair out and sat down just staring at the box in front of me. I took a sip of my coffee and decided it needed something a bit stronger for what I was about to embark on this chilly December day. I poured about a quarter of the coffee out and replaced it with some whiskey. Returning to the table, I took a drink, and removed the lid. There on top was a crime scene photo of a girl, a very young girl by the looks of it, laying haphazardly on what appeared to be a concrete ground, sidewalk maybe. Her hair matted with blood, but I could tell it was light in color, blonde perhaps or strawberry blonde. The blood gave an orange color. Her hands perfectly positioned across her chest, almost prayer-like, her body nude, legs crossed at the ankles. No other visible injuries could be seen from the photograph. I picked it up and held it to the light. There was writing on the back of it. Typical of Sam's M.O of taking notes. The letter A.M and a time of 15:45 along with a date of October 12 written in black sharpie.

I looked back at the photo again and noted the flash of the camera as well as the time stamp showing a 10:00pm time and wondered why Sam wrote 3:45 pm on the photograph when it was taken at night. Putting the photo back in the box I went over to the kitchen drawer and took out a notepad and pen and jotted down the first of many notes I would be discussing with Sam. Walking back over to the table, the cell phone in my pocket rang. The number displayed was an Oklahoma area code, recognizing the very familiar number, I reluctantly answered.

"Lieutenant Hansen, let me guess, Sam?'

" Good morning to you too, Johanna. I am great, thanks for asking."

" How did I know you would be calling me, Lue? Listen, I told Sam I would take a look, I am not coming back."

Lieutenant Hansen let out a heavy sigh," I knew you were going to say that, but that is not why I called."

"Ok then why"

" I sent you an email, did you get it?"

"Umm I don't know, I don't make it a habit anymore to answer emails when I am not at work."

I walked over to my couch, sat down and opened my laptop that was sitting on my coffee table. A few clicks and I was in my gmail account.

" Ahh yes, I see it now, Urgent from Lieutenant Hansen, yes, I have received it."

" Listen , Johanna, this case… it's, well …"

" What ? Just spit it out already."

" Open the email and you'll see."

Clicking the link in his email a video popped up and at first , it was just black, I had to turn the volume up to hear clicking noises and what sounded like heavy breathing. This went on for about a minute before a picture slowly emerged. Panning across a well kept empty room aside from a chest of drawers, landing on the foot of a bed, slowly panning up the bed to reveal feet spread and bound to the bed posts , then legs with blood streaming down them presumably from her vaginal area, up a torso covered in a Nirvana t-shirt, and finally a familiar face, only this portrayed a very alive Jane Doe. Her hands were above her head and duct taped to the head board posts. Her face twisted in horror, but not gagged.

She looked at the camera person in intense and extreme horror as the camera person continued to film her. She never made a sound, not a whimper, not a whisper. She just stared at him. I told the Lieutenant I would call him back as I continued to watch. The camera person walked over to the chest of drawers, opened the top drawer and retrieved a pipe from it. Positioning the camera on the top of the dresser to where it pointed to the bed to see her again laying there, silent and motionless. Above the headboard was a family portrait taken in a manner where the family was looking down at the bed in utter awe and admiration. A sick sentiment of the deranged mind behind this heinous act. This is the first time the perp comes into view. Clad in nothing but white boxer briefs and a ski mask, visibly a male as his manhood protrudes from his boxers, walks the pipe over to the bed and instrumentally begins to rape Jane with the pipe as he pleasures himself. Slamming my laptop shut, I vomited there on my living room floor. Something I haven't done since I was a rookie some 20 years ago. Shaken, I struggled to stand. Once upright, I decided that my whiskey doesn't need coffee in it anymore, and required a bigger glass. Downing one glass, I poured another and dialed Sam's number.

" Johnnie?'

" I can't leave, but how soon can you get here?"

" Open your front door."

Stunned, but not the least bit surprised, I walked over to the door still holding my phone to my ear. Opening it, I was greeted with his famous come kiss me smile I absolutely came to loathe.

" Sam"

" Hello Detective…" He started as he continued to flash that damn smile.

" Not anymore." I objected and opened my door wider so he could step in.

" Nice, I see you finally unpacked." he said as he let himself in, scouting my place.

" You son of a bitch!" I exclaimed

" Nice to see you too Johnnie." he answered, his smile fading as he sat his bag down on the floor.

 "Whiskey in the same spot?" he asked as he walked into the kitchen and poured himself a glass.

I stood in front of my door a little longer before letting out a sigh and following him into my kitchen.

" You haven't called." I stated

He nodded over his drink, sat it down, leaned against the counter and folded his hands across his chest.

"Neither have you.' He responded

" Yes, well, I have my reasons." I countered as I retrieved my drink from the coffee table and sat down on my couch.

" Have you seen the video?" I asked

Sam poured another drink holding it in one hand and scratching his forehead for answers with the other, he walked over and sat down next to me in my overstuffed chair.

" Which one?" he asked

"Which…" I started in utter horror but again not surprised that there were others.

"Jesus Christ ! What the hell have you gotten me into Sam?"

He sat up, downed his drink and sat the glass on the coffee table. Scooting closer to me he replied, "I'm sorry Johnnie, but I had to. He leaves these videos in the victims."

" Um what? What do you mean, *in them* ? You only told me there was one vic."

" No I did not, I told you there was one I needed help identifying, not that there was only one vic."

I could feel my blood pressure skyrocketing. Pissed I stood up abruptly, my leg bumping the coffee table and tumbling over the glasses, thankfully they were empty.

" You son of a bitch!" Almost yelling this time

" Yes, you keep telling me that." He said matter of factly

" Screw you Sam, you could have told me."

" Yes, I could have, but I knew if I told you everything over the phone you wouldn't have agreed to even look."

"Screw you." I said again and sat down angrily

"How many?" I asked

Sam sat back in his chair and swung his left ankle over his right knee and tapped his fingers on his shoe.

" How many?" I asked again through gritted teeth

" Six." He reluctantly said

"Motherfucker!" I yelled

" I am retired, I said I never wanted to do this again, not after the Lake Hefner strangler. " I exclaimed

"I know Johnnie, I know. I can't express how sorry I am about this, but you're the best at this. No one else can even begin to touch your skills or expertise. Believe me. I couldn't see any other way. I wasn't even the one that suggested you, Leu did. Matter of fact I protested against it. Even bringing up the Hefner Lake Strangler incident."

" Incident?' I asked bewildered at the notion he would dismiss it as an incident.

He pursed his lips and blew hard out of his nose, lowered his head and responded," You know what I meant, I didn't have a better word. I'm sorry."

" You keep saying that, stop apologizing." I said

I stood up, threw my hair in a bun securing it with the hair tie I had on my wrist.

" Are you hungry?" I asked as I walked over to the door, grabbed my jacket and car keys.

" Um yea sure I can eat." Sam responded

" Good, grab your files I know you have in your briefcase and come on." I demanded and walked out of my front door. He followed suit and we rode silently to my favorite little cafe. One I have used to go over tax documents and investigative reports while letting my food go cold.

" Well there she is. I was wondering when you would show up today?' Jean, short and fluffy as she would say, the waitress exclaimed as we entered the cafe.

" Oh and who is this cool drink of water, I do say JJ this one might be a keeper?!" she excitedly asked

Laughing, Sam smiled and introduced himself as Detective Sergeant Sam Lyons. Not the least bit shameful at all. Ever the boastful.

" Um Yes Jean, we have some business to do, can I have my usual and is my booth available?" I asked as I ushered Sam away from Jean's means 'well prying'.

" Of course Sugar, I don't let anyone sit in it, reserve only for you." She replied as I led Sam to the back of the cafe to the only semi enclosed booth of the establishment.

" She seems nice." Sam inquired

" Yes, well nice and meddlesome." I countered as I sat facing the door. Jean walked over and inquired about what Sam wanted and to pour coffee. Once alone I started with the questions.

" When was the first vic discovered?" I asked as I opened packets of sugar and creamer and disposed of the contents into my coffee cup.

" The first one was discovered on June 3. An elderly couple was babysitting their 5 year old twin grandsons when one of them wandered off and came back screaming there was a hurt lady in the trees. The grandmother called it in. She was alive, but died two days later in the hospital. She died from an infection a foreign object inserted into her vaginal cavity and internal complications. That is when we discovered the first video. "

" Jesus… " I said as I shook my head. Sam went to say more and pull out the files from his briefcase. I stopped as I spotted Jean rounding the corner balancing our breakfast in her hands. Thanking her, she shot me a nod and Sam a wink. Shaking my head and laughing, I joked and asked, " Isn't she a bit old for you?"

Laughing he nodded and coily answered," Yes well I have been broadening my horizons lately.'

Rolling my eyes I set to eat my breakfast, or at least attempt to. Sam slid a case file across the table and tucked it under my plate.

"Jesus, can I at least get a bite or two in?" I asked as I wiped my mouth and sat back against the booth and took the file from under my plate. In it it contained the same photograph or at least the same pose as the Jane Doe. This girl too had what appeared to be light colored hair, clean aside from the blood from her head.

" She has been identified as Sara Leonard, a 19 year old UCO Pre Law student from Tulsa. Father MIA, mother is a traveling nurse out of Tulsa. She was last seen at the Edmond public library May 29 at 1930 by her study partner and roommate, Joanie Jacobs. Joanie reports that she left Sara around 1930 to go to work. She asked Sara if she wanted her to send Jason, Joanie's brother to pick her up later. Sara declined. Said she would walk as her apartment was not far from the library." Sam explained

" She doesn't own a car? " I asked

Shaking his head, he answered, " No, she rides a bike everywhere, but that day Joanie had driven them to the library."

" Boyfriend? " I asked

" Girlfriend." he answered.

" Mother confirmed she was in a relationship with Emily Hill. Had been since junior year of highschool. Mother also said that she did date Aaron

Watson from 8th grade until he died in a car accident their sophomore year. Emily was in Europe with family for the summer."

" Ok so, are we looking at a hate crime ?" I asked

" I don't think so, Sara is the only one that was gay." He answered

" Ok so anyone one say if she was having any problems with anyone, a stalker, someone who thought they could 'turn her back straight.' I asked

" No, nothing like that. Everyone said she led a quiet life, Emily lived with her and Joanie part time, everyone got along well. However, I spoke with Emily when she returned from Europe and she said that Sara had been preoccupied , her word, with something but she told Emily that she was worried about her tuition because her mom was having financial issues."

He took out a stack of photographs of all girls, all light colored hair, all posed the same way.

" This one is Eliza Mayes, 26 year army reservist, mother of a one year old baby boy. Last seen July 5, found July 9th by a dog walker at Overholser Lake early that morning. Eliza joined the military after high school, one tour in Afghanistan, wanted to pursue a career in criminal justice, left active duty at age 24 and enlisted in the reserves to attend college at OBU. Eliza too was found alive, died enroute to the hospital, video tape was found during the autopsy lodge in her rectum. The cause of death was blunt force sexual trauma that caused internal bleeding. Eliza is married to an Air Force officer Lieutenant John Mayes, who is currently deployed to Kuwait, stationed at Tinker Air Force base. I did video chat with him extensively, and learned that he deployed the day after she was reported missing. He was a very high person of interest until this one. Justine Clemmons. "

He placed a third photo on top of Eliza's and tapped it.

" Justine is a 24 year old gas station worker, single mother of twin girls. Works as a manager for seven eleven on SE 23rd street. She was last seen July 10 when she handed over the keys to the safe to the overnight manager when she realized she still had them in her pocket after she had gotten home. She dropped them off on her way to Rose State College where she is enrolled as a nursing student and takes night classes. She was found by a security guard, Malik Griffin, 35, doing rounds at the Crossroads mall. She was displayed in the middle of the parking lot. How he missed her initially is beyond me. He is also a person of interest based on that fact alone. He claims he saw a dark colored late model sedan leaving the parking lot shortly before he found her. Blacked out windows, didn't get a license plate."

" Sounds like college aged, blonde women are his cup of tea." I said as I flagged Jean for a refill of coffee. Sam threw his napkin over the photos as Jean filled both cups.

"Anything else I can get ya'll ?' Jean asked.

"Um, a couple slices of your famous pie to go Jean please and the check." I replied.

" Of course sugar, comin' right up."

" I think we better continue this conversation over a full belly and some pie, eat up." I told Sam as I dove into my bacon and blueberry pancakes. Sam put the photos back into his briefcase. I ate about half of mine before I asked him how long he was going to be in town for.

" I drained my vacation and Lieu gave me his, so about two months give or take." He answered.

" Seriously?!" I asked shocked at that revelation

"Um no, Lieu is pissed I am here honestly, wasn't too keen on bringing you on board either, but decided to give me a week at best."

" A week?" I was still blown away by it all.

" Yes well, I did have some leave saved so I took the week he offered and my leave so you have me for three weeks total." He responded by opening his hands in a gesture of ambivalence.

" Well shit, um ok I guess then we better get to work." I said as I threw a twenty on the table and gathered the files I had and stood.

" You coming or what?" I asked him.

I made him drive back to my place and I thanked him and sent him on his way. Against his infectious smile and the throbbing in my groin, I shoved him out of the door and left him on my front porch. How long he stood there before he gave up, I haven't a clue; if I was going to do this, I did not need his distraction. His incessant questions and alluring eyes. Nope not going to get caught in that again. Or at least that is what I keep telling myself. Seeing him takes me back to a place I do not want to return. Or do I? Shaking this thought out of my head, tossing the files on my table and pouring myself a drink, I found myself drifting back to the last time I saw him. He showed up here shortly after I moved here, feigning his affection, but I could smell the whiskey under his breath and his wife's perfume. Soaked from the torrential rains of a South Carolina summer and I wanted him, I always wanted him, but his wife did not deserve the disrespect so I always kept my distance. But that night, the whiskey on his breath mixed with mine and I gave in to his eyes, his hands, his lips on my body. I let all my self respect go and I gave in. I can still feel how his silk tongue moved over my body so methodically, like he already knew where all my sweet spots were. Fuck! Downing the drink and pouring another, I sat down at the table and dove into the box.

Opening the lid I am greeted once again by the mysterious photo with the encrypted message on the back and I started a ' to ask Sam' list and my own list and notes. This box, this medium, brown, evidence box held secrets. Secrets of a life lived and lost, secrets of a psychopath and his sick, sadistic mind. A box of love lost, broken hearts, sexual deviance afflictions, of murder.

Under the photo was a brown accordion folder.I have no doubt contained the file on Jane Doe and her autopsy report, but that is not going to help. At least nor right now. I needed to see her, I needed to sense her. I put the folder to the right of the box and kept digging. A brown paper bag labeled evidence one was next and I took it out and sat it down in front of the box. I continued this ritual of removing paper and plastic bags of evidence until each piece was carefully placed in a counter clock work circle around the box. Satisfied with the arrangement, I turned my attention to my altar, retrieved my prayer beads, lit the candle, and offered a prayer of clarity and sight. I never ask for answers, that is foolish to assume I would even get them, I ask for clarity to understand what I see before me and sight to see the whole picture. Only then can I even begin to find a righteous direction.

Kneeling on my prayer pillow I recite my intent and allow myself to be completely relaxed. A relaxed mind is a clear mind. I took in four deep breaths each held for four seconds and slowly released on the same count . On the last breath I began my prayer, exhaling I noticed the air shifted and a cold filled my lungs. A tingling sensation entered my legs and crept up my spine. Creating goose bumps all over my body. Focusing, I made my intent clear and precise, not faltering on my words, even though I could hear the shake in them. The cold settled in my bones making it difficult for me to breathe. Pain seared through my bones so I took my breathing deeper to cushion the blow. The cold never gets easier no matter how much I anticipate it. It hurts as much now as it did the first time I felt it. Icy fingers caressing my bones like hot barbed wire. It has taken its toll on my body both physically and mentally. Each time a new scar, each time a new pain.

I finished my prayer and lowered my head. Taking a deep breath in, I welcomed the cold, the clarity and the sight. Placing my prayer beads in their resting place; I place my hands on the ground on either side of my knees I was kneeling on, exhaling I cringed as I pushed myself up off my knees crying out against the cold that was settled there. From my knees, to my feet, and standing straight up, each movement harder and colder than the last. Standing straight up I take another big breath in, eyes still closed , centering the cold. 'Let's go to work'. I whisper to myself returning to the table of evidence. I carefully take the first paper bag and slowly open it. I slowly bring out the first piece, neatly placed in a plastic ziplock baggie; the black Nirvana t-shirt with small pieces of it missing,have been cut for testing, which tells me this evidence has already been processed. I unfolded it and held it out at arms length, admiring its holy facade of death. I brought it to my nose and a sweet exotic smell entangled in my nose. Her perfume perhaps? I turned the shirt and sniffed again, the same sweet smell hit first, already a memory scent in my brain, but so did something else. I pulled back , cleared my olfactory senses and smelled again. A pungent, musky, aroma filled my nostrils. I closed my eyes to concentrate on the smell, trying to place it. Trying to envision what the smell looked like. Blood? No, blood was a musky sweet smell, not a stinging pungent smell. Urine! This son of a bitch pissed on his victims, as if he didn't already humiliate them enough. I dropped the shirt back on the table and scrambled for my phone. Unlocking it and scrolling through my contacts until my finger landed on Sam's number. Hesitating, staring at his name on the screen for a moment, I hit the call button and on the first ring he answered.

" Sam!" I all but yelled into the phone.

" Johnnie, what's wrong?' His rugged sleepy voice sent an ache in my groin and I had to pick up the shirt again to concentrate.

" Did the lab test for urine on the clothes?"

" What? Ugh, I'm sure they tested for all bodily fluids. Why?' The tone in his voice let me know he was more awake and was probably sitting up in his bed wearing nothing but his boxer shorts. I had to shake my head to get that image out of my head.

" Do you have those lab results?"

" Umm, yea Johnnie, I have it here in my briefcase, you rushed me out before I could give it to you."

Bastard! I felt the heat rise and sting my cheeks, not enough to thaw out the cold that has set in my bones, but enough to warm the ache in my groin. He knew damn well what he was doing and oh did he do it well.

' Would you like me to bring them over Johnnie?' The tone in his voice told me he was smiling and the beast between his legs was beginning to swell

Son of a bitch! I lowered the phone to my side and threw my head back, I wanted to scream yes! At the top of my lungs and wait for him naked, instead I took a deep breath, closed my eyes and brought the phone back to my ear.

" Johnnie? Are you there? Hello?" I heard him say as I put the phone to my ear. '

" Yes I'm here, sorry, um yes I want you to bring it to me, but not tonight. I need some sleep. I will see you in the morning. And for fuck sakes, I can't help you if you don't give me everything." With that I hung up and tossed my phone on the table. Slamming my hands on the table, causing the evidence and the box to shift from their resting places. Pissed, I took out a notebook and began to write down the notes I had floating in my head. I went through each piece of evidence carefully, meticulously. Each one another piece to the puzzle I was putting together in my head. I had placed the box on the floor to have room on my table to spread the evidence out, each carefully placed in an order I felt was relevant in the sequence of events. I bent to pick it up when I did not grab at the handles but the lid, my grip caused the lid to pop up aggressively and something went flying from it landing on the kitchen chair. A newspaper clipping with the crime scene photo front and center of it, with Jane's left arm and right leg sticking out of the sheet covering her body as well as slivers of her hair. Reporters are leeches, but this photograph was too good and too close to be any of that of a cell phone or camera from a reporter. Someone leaked crime scene photos. I placed the clipping next to the videotape on the table and jotted down on my notepad to ask about the leaked photos and if there were any more leaked.

    The chime on my grandfather clock told me it was 2 a.m and decided I should at least lay down. Doubting I would actually sleep, I decided a hot bath and a gummy would help to relax enough to maybe get an hour or two. Sitting on the side of the tub, I watched the water pour into the tub as the steam from it rose and crept up like fog around a tree. Hypnotic in its steamy sarcophagus I found myself drifting into an abyss of memories. Screams filled my thoughts as the last crime scene I worked danced behind my eyes and pain seared through my body. Blue lights took over my pupils and my daughter's body took shape under the water in the tub. Mesmerized by the sight, I couldn't take my eyes off of her floating in the tub. I drove my hands into the water and grabbed a hold of her, screams echoing in my ears, reverberating against the waterlogged walls. Clutching at her drenched cold body I tried desperately to pull her up out of the tub and onto the floor, she kept slipping through my arms and sinking deeper into the water. Hysterics crawled up my legs like ants on a fence post, stinging every nerve on their way up. I yelled out from the pain causing me to once again lose my grip on her. I plummeted head first into the water striking it on the bottom of the porcelain tub, hot, white, darkness took over as water filled my lungs.

"Johnnie? Wake up! Come on Johnnie! " Sam yelled as he wiped my soaked hair from my face and tapped my face. He placed his head against my chest and felt the rise and fall of it.

"Come on now baby, wake up!' he pleaded

I could hear him, but I couldn't move. My mind screaming at my body to move, wiggle, something, but I laid there listening to this man beg for the universe to let me go and come back to him. I felt a twitch in my left hand and my fingers began to move. The ants crawled up each finger one by one as I slowly inched them off the floor, searching for his face. He noticed it as my arm slowly raised up and he took it fiercely into both of his hands and kissed them. Letting out a sigh of relief. He kissed it a few more times and placed it on my stomach, tucked his arms under me and lifted me into them. Kissing my head on the way up.

" Sam?' I said in a scratchy voice.

" Shh don't talk, it's ok I got you." Sam responded as he walked with me cradled in his arms into my room. Laying me gently on the bed. He retrieved the blanket that was tucked neatly at the foot of the bed and covered me. He knelt down next to the bed and held my hand to his lips. I could feel his breath against my knuckles as he blew in and out. He kissed them again as I drifted out of consciousness again.

The light stung my eyes even behind the lids and I winced against it as I slowly opened them. It took a moment to orient myself and Iaid there staring up at my ceiling, in a weird state of lucidity and confusion. The ceiling fan slowly turned and I watched it spin trying to recall how I came to be in my bed in the first place. The last thing I remember was getting ready for a bath. Snoring broke my attention on the slow rotation of the fan and jolted straight up, and to the left of me hunched over in a chair, one hand flopped over his stomach the other propping his chin up, was Sam. Furious, I went to kick him awake, but paused and just sat on the edge of the bed and watched him for a moment. He was dressed in jogging pants and a OSU sweat shirt, fucking pokes, his shoes were untied and his legs stretched out awkwardly and spread enough I could see the outline of what sweats so generously reveal. I knew this look all too well and knew he had been running. I closed my eyes and reminisced on how good he smelled after a run. That sweet aroma of his shower gel and sweat. His salty neck and how good it tasted on my tongue. Shaking my head, I swore under my breath, and nudged him with my foot.

He jolted awake and cleared his throat. He smiled at me and leaned forward in a muscle memory attempt to kiss me. Awkwardly, I moved my head back. Lowering his head, he silently apologized.

" Good morning." I said

" 'mornin." He responded

" Mind telling me why you're in my house, much less my room?" I asked

He snapped his head to the side and his brow formed a confused arched. " Um you don't remember calling me?' He asked quizzically

Shaking my head, I shrugged. He stood up, towering over me, the generosity staring me in my face, I cleared my throat and as nonchalantly as I possibly could, scooted back to the middle of my bed. Realizing this, he sat back down again in the chair and leaned closer to me.

" Well, I went on a run last night after you called about the lab results. I couldn't sleep. I was headed back to my hotel, I don't know about 3 am, when you called, hysterical, screaming something about Amaria, and the killer, I don't know ,you weren't making any sense. So I ran over. Your door was wide open, the kitchen a mess and I found you in the bathroom on the floor unconscious. The tub was flooding the floor."

Hearing this threw me into a whirlwind. Hearing him say her name threw me into a bigger one. I swung my legs around to the other side of the bed and stood up. Excited realization struck a chord in my gut and sent a familiar memory to my psyche.

" Oh my fucking goddess!" I exclaimed, causing Sam's eyes to go wide and stand as well. I practically ran out of the room. Confused and curious, Sam followed suit. I made a beeline to the couch where my laptop was still open and laying haphazardly on it. I paused for a hot second at the state my living room was in. It was completely trashed. Shaking it off, I tapped the screen to wake the sleeping beast illuminating a paused video on the perp holding the pipe 'he' just violated Jane with.

    I enlarged the image on the mask covered face and focused in on the eyes. I swiveled the laptop around to show Sam who had sat on the edge of the coffee table.

" What do you see?" I asked, looking at him wide eyed. His brow furrowed and he looked at me in confused and concerned manner before turning his attention to the screen.

Sighing, he replied," I see a masked perp's cold blue eyes."

" And?" I asked. " Look harder." I prompted

He took the laptop and moved from the coffee to my oversized chair, placing it in his lap. He zoomed the image in and out until his eyes went wide.

" Oh fuck!" He exclaimed

I nodded my head and I could feel a shit eating grin come on my face. There, just below the right eye a small blemish can be seen. The tip of an all too familiar birthmark.

" There's no way it's him, Johnnie, we watched him be executed!" He exclaimed

" I never said it was him." I responded

" I need those lab results, and I need to see those other videos, including his." I urged

Sam closed the laptop and studied my face a minute before speaking. He didn't get the chance to utter a word before I interjected.

" I know what you're thinking and what you're going to say, but I am fine. Better even. Because now, I am going to make damn sure that bastardly bloodline ceases to exist."

He sighed heavily and let his head fall some before he spoke. " Ok, but is it cool if I shower first and get some food? Can't end bastardly bloodlines on an empty stomach, and um…You might want to put some clothes on as well."

Looking down I realized I was naked aside from my very thin robe that was not secured at all and all my lovely bits were hanging out for the world to see. Embarrassed, I could feel my cheeks go hot as I quickly closed my robe and folded my arms around my chest to secure it. Laughing, he said," You forget I have seen it all before, and I have to admit, the extra weight is umm.. So very hot, I love it." He winked at me and headed for the door.

I watched him walk away, and felt that ache between my legs heat up. My cheeks stung with embarrassed heat. I stood up and tied my robe and walked behind him to the door. He swung open the door and turned to me, not expecting me to be behind him, he smiled and kissed my cheek, leaving me once again craving more.

An hour later, we were greeted by Jean and her chipper excitement to see us together again. I shook my head and warded off her matchmaking innuendos as she brought us our breakfast and refilled our coffee. When I knew she would not be back for awhile, I asked Sam for the lab results. I scanned them over my pancakes while nibbling on bacon. I could feel his eyes on me, but I dared not look up. Cheeks still burning from the naked exposure of the morning. Finding what I was looking for, I excitedly looked up.

"There!" I pointed with a greasy finger, smudging the paper as I handed it to him. He took it from me, puckered his lips at my greasy fingerprint and examined what I was pointing at.

"Holy shit." He said as he laid the document on the table and dug into his briefcase. Rambling at the same time, " I saw something in one of the other vic's lab results, and at first I figured it was just hers and not the perp's. It was an anomaly, the only thing that made this particular girl different from the rest. Everything else is identical except this."

He found what he was looking for and handed the file to me. I wiped my hands and took it from him. Opening the document I scanned the report before my eyes landed on what they were meant to see. " She was pregnant? " I inquired. Shaking his head he put an autopsy report over what I was looking at, she had been a he.

" His name was Jameson Stuart and at 17 he came out to his parents, and at 21 had reassignment surgery and became Jaquelyn Stuart. A 24 year old pre-law student at Cameron University. The day before graduation she was reported missing by her boyfriend Harrison Malone, three days later she was found on the running track of Eisenhower High School by the cross country girls team on their morning practice. Same M.O. The difference was she was covered in urine. The other's hair was the only place where urine was found. The lab assumed the same thing as I did, because the other urine tested did not give a positive pregnancy test. In fact, they had high levels of testosterone in them. We assumed the perp was a juicer."

The smile on my face grew bigger as what he just told me confirmed my suspicions.

"I know who the perp is, better yet I know who Jane is!" I said as I stacked the papers and placed them back into the file folder. Hastily I I stood up and threw some money on the table and told Sam we had to leave. He shuffled out of the booth and haphazardly followed behind me dropping his briefcase on the floor causing patrons to look in our direction. He smiled sheepishly and excused his clumsiness. I couldn't help but notice how sexy he looked embarrassed and stumbling over himself, I giggled under my breath.

" So let me get this straight.." Sam said while dodging tables and chairs through the restaurant and out the door behind me. " We are actually on the same page ??' I stopped abruptly at the passenger side door of his rental and cut him a sharp look over my shoulder, " We were always on the same page, it's just you always took longer to get there than I did." I responded sarcastically as I gave him a wink and opened the car door and sat down. Looking up at him I gave him a sly smile as I closed the door. He stood there a half of a second interpreting what I just did. Damn did he drive me crazy and I wondered if I did the same to him.

"Where are we headed now?' He asked as he settled in behind the steering wheel. As I secured my seat belt and watched him fumble with the keys, I scanned every inch of him, wanting to take him right then and there in that car, on that road, in front of that diner. He must have felt my energy surge through him as his hand froze at the ignition and he hesitated to turn it over. Slowly he looked up at me and met my devilish eyes on him. He didn't get a chance before my tongue was down his throat and my hands down his pants, stroking all of his generosity. I couldn't help myself. An epiphany on a case always made me hot and doing it with him, even hotter.

His hands were immediately wrapped in my hair as he latched on with fierce intensity. His dominance exuberates with every lash of his tongue against mine. His grip on my hair tighter with every stroke of my hand. His other hand found its way around my neck and my body screamed and ached for his pulsing generosity. I felt him swell bigger and harder in my hand. His grip on my hair and neck tighter as my pulse quickened he let go of my neck and I took him in my mouth. Caressing him with my tongue, stroking him against my cheeks. His legs trembled and his hands in my hair eased and tightened with each stroke of my mouth and flick of my tongue until he exploded. Rocking his head back he let out a guttural groan of satisfaction.

" Damn it girl!" He exclaimed as he cleaned himself up and secured his generosity into the comfort of his pants. Laughing I wiped the corner of my mouth and tapped the dashboard. A signal for him to get moving. " Where to?" He asked again. " My place, I need to pack a bag and get a plane ticket. I'm going to go see an old friend."

With that he turned over the ignition and we drove in silence the 3 miles back to my home. Pulling into my driveway, he sat awkwardly staring at my garage door. Hand on the door handle, I spoke without looking at him, " My turn." Without another word he opened his door to finish opening mine. He stood blocking my way out and looked up at him with curious intent. His generosity I could see pulsing against his right pant leg. His looked screamed,' about time' as he pushed me against the console, and in one swift move had my pants off and legs over his shoulders, taking me in his mouth, not giving on fuck about who saw what. Hell neither did I.

His tongue was pure silk. His hands held my legs against his shoulders as I wrapped them around his head. His moaning caused a vibrational pull with his tongue against my soul that sent an electric shock through my entire body. I grasped at anything and everything I could, squirming under his hot exotic mouth. He locked down on my thighs and held me there as his tongue lashed viciously until my body turned itself inside out releasing a sleeping demon that had been laying dominant for so very long. I shook under his spell and my legs twitched as he gently licked every drop I gave him. Damn I have missed that tongue. FUCK!

Pulling myself together as he helped me pull my pants back up, he laughed as he noticed an old couple across the street on their porch drinking their coffee. The gentleman raised his cup to Sam as his wife shook her head and smacked him with her newspaper. Sam blushed as he laughed as he nodded at the old man and helped me out of the car. Looking over at the couple I gave a smile and a nod as I walked into my house. The disarray from the night before still strewn around my living room. Echoes of visions flew around me causing my head to swim and I stumbled back bumping into Sam. " Whoa, easy Johnnie, you ok?" Sam asked as he caught me. " Umm yea, I just got a little light headed." I said as I took a deep breath and collected myself as best as I could. I pushed off of him and wobbly walked towards my room.

" Hey Sam!" I called out ." Do you mind throwing my laptop and my notes in my go bag, it's in the coat closet by the door?' I asked as I entered my room and started throwing clothes on my bed. I dialed the airline and put a one way flight on my Amex card, simultaneously texting my work and taking the remainder of my vacation time. As I finished booking my flight, my assistant texted back with an angry emoji face cursing me at leaving him to the mercy of the 'dumbass staff'. I smiled as I sent him back a kissy face and an' I'll be back soon,' before tossing my phone in the pile of clothes. The beauty of being a boss, I don't need permission to do what the hell I want.

Walking into my bathroom, I was greeted with a wet floor. Confused as to why my bathroom floor was covered in wet towels and puddles. My shower curtain haphazardly pushed aside and blood ran down the side of it fading as it went down the side and pooled near the drain. Horror ripped through my veins as I tried to make sense of it all. Flashes of light flickered behind my eyes as Amaria danced in them. I turned on the hot water in the shower and let it wash away the blood. I watched it swirl around the tub before emptying down the drain. My hand instinctively went to the top of my head and winced at the pain from the knot on it. Remembering the events of last night and the message I was given. Telling me exactly what I needed to know. I stripped my clothes, got in the shower and let the heat take me over, cleansing my mind and my body. Preparing for what is to come next.

   Sam was sitting on the edge of my bed looking at a photo I had on my nightstand of Amaria and I, senior prom. The very night she went missing. He looked up at me as I walked from the bathroom towel drying my hair. His eyes were misty and solemn. I half smiled and took it from him. I wiped the dust from it with the corner of my towel and set it back in its place on my nightstand. Sam watched me intently, took my hand, and sat me down next to me. Bringing my hand up to his lips, kissing it gently. Tears welled up in my eyes and burned as they rolled down my cheeks. Sam looked up at me, eyes glossy and wet, he used his other hand to wipe my cheek. I leaned into it and let his thumb caress my cheek.

" I'm sorry Johnnie, I should have been here for you more." Sam began. I kissed his palm and brought it from my face. Shaking my head, because I knew why he wasn't. I knew the predicament of me keeping Amaria had put him in, I also knew the pain he felt when he found her body. I sniffed and tried to get up, he held onto my hand causing my body to jerk back towards him as I tried to stand. I protested, but he stood and wrapped me in his arms. Kissing the top of my head, the flood gates opened and I broke. Ugly and completely I broke. He held me there as I relentlessly sobbed and shook in his arms. He shushed and rocked me. Saying how he was sorry and he loved me over and over again.

He sat us both down on the edge of the bed again, and he continued to hold and rock me gently. I regained control of my senses and had stopped crying, but I stayed nestled in his arms a little longer until he jokingly said," Detective Mallory, If you do not get up and secure proper clothing I am going to have to arrest you for indecent exposure and arousal of a police officer." I snorted and punched him in his gut, causing him to laugh and let go of me to rub his stomach. " Damn, I see your punch is still powerful." He laughed as I stood and walked over to my dresser. He watched me for a moment, stood, adjusted his swelling pants and exited my room. I smiled and shook my head, letting my towel drop. I choose yoga pants and an oversized sweatshirt, my favorite flying clothes. Oklahoma will be colder than it was here, probably with snow on the ground; so I made sure to wear a t-shirt underneath, donned long socks that fit over my pant legs and my favorite fuzzy UGG boots. Satisfied, I secured a hair tie around my wrist and met Sam, who was literally waiting outside my bedroom door.

    He smiled, shook his head, and said, " Some things never change, you're going to ca…"

" Catch my death with wet hair?" I finished as I smiled at him and walked around him into the kitchen. I started putting all the evidence I had laid out on the table back into its box. Careful to put the back in the order they were in, working backwards. Sam watched me, he knew this song and dance and knew to not interfere with my ' shenanigans' as he called them. My 'shenanigans' have proven many cases, too many, so he has learned to let me do me. Once everything was back in the box, in their original order, I secured the lid with box tape I found in my kitchen drawer and slid the box towards Sam. He lifted his left hand, revealing he had been holding my go bag this whole time. I smiled and held my hand out to take it from him so he could take the box instead.

" Ready?' I asked. He nodded, took the box, and headed for the door. I followed behind, scanning the room once more making sure I wasn't forgetting anything. I unplugged the coffee pot and made sure the kitchen window was closed, locked the back door and headed for the front. As I approached the front door I was hit with a freezing cold draft, a flash of light, and a sickening smell that made me lightheaded enough to stumble. An all too familiar smell that filled my lungs and stung my nose. I caught myself on the doorframe, slid onto the shoe chair, closed my eyes and steadied myself. *'I know, I am coming, I will help you, but you must let me.'* I said under my breath. I took in three slow deep breaths, cleared my nostrils of the smell and slowly rose to my feet. I stood a moment to make sure my legs were steady enough for walking. I opened my eyes, nodded at nothing and walked out into the sun, greeted by the Carolina cold.

Sam was patiently waiting, leaning against the passenger car door. He had placed the box in the backseat and was smoking a cigarette. " I thought you gave up that shit?" I asked as I handed him my bag to be put in the backseat as well. He flicked the butt on the ground and stomped it out with his shoe. Nodding as he blew the smoke out. " I did." he responded as he opened the car door for me and placed my bag in the back, hoisting it over the front seat. I gave him a look and sat down in the car. I reached for the door but he beat me to it and closed it. He smiled at me through the glass and walked behind the car and over to the driver side. I looked up at my house, saw Amaria standing in the window, I whispered,*" I am going to get them all this time baby girl."*

The ride to the airport was quiet, but not the awkward and uneasy kind. I read over the remaining case files, making mental notes that I would put in my notebook when we weren't moving at ridiculous speed. Sam always did drive nauseatingly fast, even reading was beginning to make my head spin. I put all the papers back in his briefcase as we entered the rental car return. We dropped the keys at the Budget car rental desk and headed for the terminal. I took the liberty of checking us in on my phone, I hate waiting in line at the ticket counter. Security was less than fun, busy for the holidays, but once we were through and sitting in our terminal with 30 minutes to spare, we could breathe a little. Sam found us some coffee,' Black three sugars and cinnamon,' he said as he handed me a hot cup of life and a blueberry crumb cake. Not surprised he remembered, yet still flattered he did, I graciously took his gifts. He sat down beside me, adjusted in his seat, took a slurp of his coffee,(he never sips anything) before asking,' So you wanna tell me who Jane is?' With a mouth full of blueberry crumb cake, I nodded and wiped my mouth. I sat my coffee and cake on the seat next to me and pulled out a large manilla envelope and handed it to him. The envelope looked like it had been through hell and back, and well, it had. It was the last case I had been working on when Amaria went missing. I tossed it aside and focused on Amaria's case. It was a missing ten year old girl, who disappeared from Crossroads Mall, Halloween 1999. She had been trunk or treating with her mom and two of her cousins when they were separated by the crowd.

Sam took the envelope from me, looked at me quizzically as he opened it and took out its contents. His face fell white when he read the name. " Johanna, are you sure?" he asked directly. Whenever he used my name like that, it meant he was horrified. I nodded and responded with," Yes I am, we never found her body. I worked on it for months, no leads, no suspects, but it was something that Marcus Orion said to me during his interrogation of Amaria's murder. He said,' trick or treat.' I never knew what that meant until now. Or maybe I did and just didn't put two and two together. I was so focused on catching my, our daughter's, killer, that I lost sight and objectivity on Cassie's."

Sam sighed, handed me back the envelope, and took out his phone. He looked at me as his phone began to ring. I could see he did not want to make that call. " Lieu? Yea its me, listen, we think we know who Jane is. " There was a long pause before Sam handed me his phone. I looked at him questioning this gesture with my eyes, I took the phone. " Lieutenant Hansen, Cassandra Morris." Is all I said before handing the phone back to Sam. He took the phone back, informed Lieutenant Hansen that we both were on the first flight to Oklahoma City. Sam put his phone back in his pocket and told me that Lieu is headed to the M.E's office to have them run DNA samples of Jane and compare to the samples we still had on ice of Cassie's.

" There's one more thing, Lieu wants you to go talk to Cassie's parents." The news of this hit me like a ton of bricks. Her parents were furious, and rightfully so, at me for how I handled their daughter's case. I was blinded by my own grief that I lost sight of theirs. This adventure home was going to be a grand one. I nodded in compliance. Sam looked at me and rhetorically asked, 'He kept her all this time, but why?' I answered anyway with, 'Julian Orion".

2

Marcus Orion was a 55 year old accountant from Broken Arrow, Oklahoma, when he was arrested. He was a successful family man with a very disturbing past and an equally disturbing dark side. He was adopted at the age of 2 by very loving parents who could not have children of their own. They adopted two more children after Marcus. Marcus was born Jared Alexander Clark, to Emily Clark and Alex Cockerel from El Paso, Texas. Alex sexually exploited Emily for his own sadistic pleasures. Marcus was the fourth pregnancy and second live birth of the glorious pair. Emily turned her trauma into an alcohol crazed band aid, and Alex turned his attention to his children. Viciously raping Marcus' sister causing permanent brain damage and sexual trauma she now resides in an assisted living facility. She and Marcus were removed from the home after this incident, but not before Alex turned his attention to Marcus. Both children suffered vicious attacks from their father and suspected the same from their mother, although that has never been proven.

Jason and Elizabeth Orion adopted Jared in a closed adoption. The Orion's changed his name and took him back to Broken Arrow, where he flourished into a seemingly healthy, successful, young man. Graduating valedictorian from OSU with an Accounting degree. It was not until he was 25 years old when an accident on a ski trip did things change. His wife suspected he was having an affair, and oh how she wished that were true now. He married his college sweetheart and they had three daughters.Julie in 1985, Eliza(after his adopted mother)in 1987, and Margaret in 1990. After his execution, Margaret felt safe enough to come out and tell her story of torment, sadistic torture, and molestation at the hands of her father.Eliza corroborated the story, Julie denied any such acts. Julie, a blue eyed, red haired, beauty, tom boy, straight 'A' student, marked undoubtedly as Marcus' daughter by the birthmark they shared below their right eyes.

Julie came out first to Eliza, then Margaret on her realization that she was a man trapped in a woman's body. She was 23 years old, in school for Nursing at Cameron. She was dating a young man by the name of Shawn when she became pregnant and met 24 year old Jaquelyn Stuart. Sam interviewed Julie, he at the time had no clue he was interviewing the killer. Julie did not want to be associated with her dad and assumed the last name of her then boyfriend Shawn Masterson. The two later married after the birth of their son, Aaron, divorced shortly after when Julie came out to Shawn. Shawn was disgusted by this notion, took Aaron and left Julie to her devices. She spiraled out of control at the loss of her son and her identity, throwing herself into transitioning from Julie Masterson to Julian Masters.

Julie was the only one to ever visit her father in prison. Records showed she was there for every visitation and stayed the entire time. She even showed up to his execution and signed in as Julian Orion. Eliza and Margaret were also in attendance, however, were shocked at the very sight of their new found brother. Eliza described Julian as cold and creepy. Margaret said her sister was no longer behind those eyes and that she was terrified of who was. I never, in a million years would have ever suspected any of those girls to become anything remotely resembling their father, but clearly I was wrong. I was too distracted by my own grief that my judgment and expertise were clouded. Julian simply got overlooked until now, a mistake I will never make again.

The flight to Oklahoma City was uneventful. Sam slept as I poured over my notes and made more during layovers and airtime. Mainly I stewed over the fact that I had to talk to Cassie's mom. The last time I saw her, she had spat in my face and expressed her undeniable grief filled hate for me. Rightfully so. I deserved it and I owned it, still does not make what I was about to do any easier. Lieutenant Hansen was there waiting for us when we landed at Will Rogers, leaning against his black tahoe smoking a cigarette. He watched me intently as I moved closer to him. His eyes danced with thoughts of admiration, guilt, excitement, and remorse. He nodded at Sam as he threw our bags into the back hatch of the tahoe. I stopped in front of him and met his gaze. I could see his eyes go misty for a moment, but he took one last drag on his cigarette and flicked it to the side, and threw his arms around me. He was a beast of a man, deep toned and huge arms. Sometimes so emotionless he could be cold and calculated, but with me in this moment, I saw a side of him I have never seen. His beastly stature melted as he squeezed me so tight, I thought I was going to burst. " Jesus Lieu, I can't breathe!" I exclaimed. His laugh boomed under the awning. He let me go and swung around to open my door. " It's just so damn good to see ya Johanna, so damn good." He said as he ushered me into the passenger side of his tahoe.

Sam climbed in behind Lieu, he must have his grandbaby as her carseat was strapped in behind me. I chuckled at Sam as he dug a baby doll from under his butt and placed it in the car seat. Lieu apologized as he climbed in behind the steering wheel. " How is Stacia?" I asked as we exited the arrivals terminal and drove out of the airport.

"Oh you know, driving me crazy as ever. Jonas deployed to Afghanistan last month, so we have been on extra grandkid duty. I know one thing, I am too damn old for babies anymore." he chuckled. " Stacia has the damn house all baby proof and ready, hell the kids 4 now, why the hell we need baby gates is beyond me, but you know Stacia." He shrugged as he turned onto I40 and we drove towards Yukon. " How are you Johanna, truly? You good?' He asked me. I took a deep breath in and let it out before I answered," I was until that knucklehead landed on my doorstep." I joked as I pointed back at Sam. " Seriously though, I have been really good. Opened up my own little boutique, mornings on the beach, it's been really good for me."

He nodded and we drove the rest of the way in silence. I still owned a house in Yukon. I rent it out in the summer, but in the winter, my brother comes and winterizes it and locks it up tight. Lieu has cars patrolling the area at night, even though I told him that was unnecessary. I had cameras installed and when my brother does his thing, he activates them so I can keep an eye on it. Still I see on my computer the Yukon Police Dept drive by and flash lights to let me know. I give a 'hello boys' to my computer and go to bed. We pulled into my driveway and the automatic flood light lit us up like the fourth of July. I squinted against it and fumbled for my phone. Typing in the code I shut it off.

"Damn Johanna!" Lieu exclaimed as he turned the car off.

" Sorry Lieu. I installed that before I left, I just forgot about it being so damn bright."

I opened the door and stood in the driveway just staring up at my dark house. Ominous in the moonlight. Steam rolling out of my nose against the cold of night. Shivering, I pulled my hoodie tight and walked up the walkway, punched the numbers on the lockbox and took out my keys. I hesitated on the lock, looked up at the camera, letting my brother know it was me. I forgot to call him. The porch light flashed two times and I slid the key in the lock and pushed open the door. The smell of dust hit my nose as I fumbled for the light switch, illuminating a room full of sheet covered furniture and a stack of mail on the door side table.

There is an unsettling calmness that settles in my gut. One that solidified the cold that settled there. I wrap my arms around my body and slowly walk into my living room. I was pulling dusty sheets off my furniture when I uncovered the coffee table and saw the cup rings on them. Laughter flashed in my ears that nearly brought me to my knees. Sitting on the couch, flashes of her danced behind my tear soaked eyes. I closed them to see her clearer, and her image sketched out before me on her phone, feet bare and gracing the edge of the very same table, her sweating glass of iced tea making yet another ring stain on the table. Her laughter as she scrolls through whatever ridiculousness that is trolling social media. A tear soaked smile donned my face as I sat there transfixed on that image forever ingrained in my thoughts. Oh God, how

I wanted to wrap her in my arms again, smell the sweet scent that was her, to hear her laugh one more time. A pressure on my thigh brought me out of the image and for a moment I thought I called her name.

" Johnnie? You alright? Did you not hear me calling you?' Sam asked as he slouched over me, hand on my thigh. I quickly wiped my face and nodded as I stood to finish uncovering the rest of the furniture. `` It's a bit cold in here". I said as I walked over to the thermostat, typed the lock box code on the keypad to unlock it and bumped the temp to 72. I could feel Sam's eyes on me as I walked away from him, I clenched my teeth and didn't turn around until I knew for sure my face wouldn't give it away.

" There!" I exclaimed as I shut the lock box.

" I am very certain that there isn't any food in this place, however, I know where there is whiskey." I said as I turned to greet the stare that was burrowing a hole right through me.

" Um actually, Johanna, I had Eli bring over some groceries. He stocked the fridge for ya." Lieutenant Hansen responded as he brought in our bags and sat them by the door.

" Ah, it explains why it's freezing in here!" I chuckled.

Lieu looked from me to Sam and back to me again. Unsure as to what to say next, he simply excused himself. Told us a car would be by to get us in the morning. I looked at Sam curiously. Confused as to why he wasn't going home to his wife. Lieu said goodnight and flashed his lights as he drove away.

" Ok Sam, spill it." I said as I walked over to him, took the sheets he was holding and began folding them. He gave his half wit smile and signed reluctantly. "Umm.." he began rubbing the back of his neck and walking around me to the bar. Pouring two tumbler glasses of whiskey, he trades me for the sheets and sets them down on a bar stool. I folded one leg under the other and sat on my loveseat. Downing the glass I handed it back to him for a refill and he obliged and sat down across from me in the same spot I just saw Amaria in. I blinked a few times to clear my sight and focused intently on Sam. He took a big drink from his glass and sat on the coffee table, adjusted in his seat. Stalled. He was stalling.

" Ok stop, what's going on?" I said impatiently

" About two years ago, Macy got sick. No one could figure out what was going on. She went to countless doctors to no avail. Finally she decided to seek advice in Dallas and contacted a specialist there. So she called, asked me if I would drive with her…"

" Um, what do you mean 'called you', where were you?" I asked him, interrupting him. He gave his half wit smile again as if to say,*' let me finish'*.

" So I agreed and cleared my schedule to take her. We had been divorced 3 years at this point. I caught her and my brother together. Guess it was my penance for you, I don't know, but I hadn't talked to either one until that point. Anyways, the specialist in Dallas ran a shit ton of tests and it was finally determined that she had a rare form of pneumonia. One that was antibiotic resistant. She was immediately put into the hospital. Horrendous lung therapies, medications, she basically withered before my eyes. I found out she had married my brother, had a baby and started to become sick shortly after giving birth. Doctors think maybe she contracted it in the hospital during childbirth. Something about the oxygen tubing."

He paused and I watched pain appear behind his eyes as they went glassy from tears. He cleared his throat and wiped his nose before continuing. " I tried calling my brother, left message after message. I later found out he had moved out after the baby was born and no one knows where he is. So I stayed until Macy's sister arrived, three hours after her sister arrived, Macy coded and was gone." He let that sentiment linger as he sat there twirling his glass slightly to make the whiskey swirl. I took a moment to wrap my head around what he just told me. Honestly, I didn't know what to say. So I didn't say anything. Classic Johanna.

" Macy's sister and my mom share custody of the baby, my brother was found in Vegas with some chick he was having an affair with online, and well Macy's lies peacefully in the ground. My brother did eventually come back, but that was only because the courts located him to terminate his rights. Fucking bastard." He angrily said as he sat his glass back down on the coffee table.

" Oh shit Sam, I'm…I'm so sorry you had to go through that. Why didn't you call me?' I asked

He looked sharply and angrily at me. Telling me I knew the answer before I even asked. I nodded and sat my glass down on the coffee table. I stood up and held out my hand. He looked up at me, sighed and took my hand. I gently tugged on him until he stood up, and I led him down the hall and into my room.

3

The sunlight beaming through a crack in my curtains woke me, I slowly opened my eyes squinting against the light. It took me a moment to remember where I was as I sat up in bed. I looked over and realized I was alone, and for half a second, thought I dreamed everything up until this point. The smell of bacon and coffee waffled through the air and a horrible, cat in heat, singing trailed behind the sweet aroma. I smiled and kicked the covers off me. I walked into the kitchen and leaned against the door. He was dancing in front of the stove, singing every word to a song that was blaring in his ears. I walked over to him and stood behind him a moment, hoping he would sense me there. When he did not, I tapped his shoulder causing him to jump and drop the spatula he was rhythmically using to scramble eggs.

Smiling, he took out his Airpods, shut off the stove and told me to sit and eat. I complied, but not before pouring me a cup of coffee. I took my coffee and my plate from the table and went into the living room. There scattered all over the coffee table were the case files and pictures. The box of Jane's evidence was sitting on the chair and the whiskey glasses were placed on the bar. I took up residency on the couch and balanced my plate on the arm of it and sat my coffee on the end table. Sam followed suit at the other end.

" Couldn't sleep?" I asked as I shoved pancake and bacon in my mouth. He shook his head before answering," Um no, not really. I mean I did for about an hour after… but then I didn't want to disturb you, so I came in here and started working."

" Anything new?" I asked

" Um, well not sure if it is new, or we just missed it. Why did he keep Cassie? Did Julian know that his dad took Cassie? Did Marcus groom and train Julian for this? None of that makes sense."

I sat my plate on the end table and nodded my understanding of what Sam was trying to say. Swallowing the remainder of my pancakes and bacon, leaving my eggs untouched, I answered." Well, maybe when we pick Julian up today for questioning, he can fill in those blanks. Do we know where he is currently?"

Sam nodded, chewing, he pointed to a pile of papers in front of me. I picked them up and leaned back against the couch. They were last known for Julian. He certainly did not try to hide. We had bank records, medical records, school records, of when he was Julie and now as Julian. Even the name of the pediatrician he used for his son, that trail of course died, when Shawn filed for divorce and moved away with Aaron.

" What I can't figure out is why he chose these particular women? Like what is the common denominator?" I asked, mainly to myself

" I mean aside from every victim having physical similarities, what was it about them that set him off ?"

Sam had finished his breakfast and scooted closer to the coffee table. He leaned over me to grab a file folder that was sticking out from under another stack of papers. He plopped it in front of me on the table. " I think this will explain that." he said as he settled back into the couch again. I opened the folder, read the first few lines and my eyes went wide. Holy shit, all of the women were members of an anti-trans group. The leader was 47 year old Maxine Yates, an OBU graduate of Theological

Studies. Ordained in the Church of Holy Sanctions. Founded by her in 2001.

    I stood up and fumbled over the chaos of papers over to our bags still sitting by the door and retrieved my laptop. I made my way back over to the couch and fired it up. Typing in the search engine 'The Church of Holy Sanctions,' and there center stage was Maxine Yates surrounded by every victim including Julie Orion. " Oh my fucking godness!" I said as I turned the computer around and showed Sam what I was looking for. Sam sat straight up and took the laptop from me. He zoomed the picture in on the image I was pointing at and there behind everyone else, deliberately placed herself there I have no doubt, was indeed, Julie Orion.
" Holy shit!" Sam exclaimed. " How did I miss that connection?"
" Easy, you weren't looking for a woman." I answered

    The adrenaline rushed through my veins and I could hear my heart beat into my ears. Jumping up, I got lightheaded and swooned back some. Sam reacted to catch me, but I steadied myself, grabbed my bag and headed for my room. I called out to Sam to finish up his breakfast. I hurriedly performed the ' three S's', well two, I didn't have time to shave. I needed that extra time to pray for strength to do what was on the agenda to do today. The text from Lieu confirming the identity of Jane as Cassie, I knew exactly what I would pray for and what I would say, implementing those thoughts to words however, would require a very focused and intentional prayer.

    In the linen closet of my master bathroom I kept a small altar of sorts. Stocked primarily with the same artifacts I had in my Carolina home. I opened the french doors and was greeted with Armaria's face. I had forgotten for a brief second about the altar being set up for guided prayers of return to me. Teary eyed I gently picked up the framed picture and wiped the dust off the face of it. Smiling, I held it to my breast and whispered a gratitude to her and placed her on the shelf below the altar. I lit the candles, spelling gratitude and intent over each of them. There was a small bottle of water standing to the right of the altar and I poured a cap full into the tuning bowl. Striking the tuning bowl with its handle. I let the tuned melody take into my ears as I closed my eyes and focused on the sound. Striking the bowl two more times, I offered my gratitude and my prayers. Allowing each tuned strike to enter with grace and exit with fortitude. When I was done, I turned on the shower and dropped three drops of essential oil into the tub and let the steam activate them. Inhaling the aromatic steam, I let my clothes fall to the floor and allowed the hot water and steam to consume me entirely. The water never felt so good. The heat soaking into my skin and thawing the cold in my gut to a bearable tolerance. I placed my forehead against the shower wall under the shower head and let the water beat down my neck and spine. Sending out the same prayer and gratitude, I cleansed my body of the night before, of the plane ride, the staleness of the house, the ache in my chest and the anger of the pain I will endure. I knew I would be doing this longer after all this is done. After the case when I return back to the comfort of my Carolina cold, but for now this will do.

A small knock brought me out of my head, I sent out a quick *'I'm almost done'* to Sam and I turned off the water and stood in the steam for a few more seconds. A hand appeared around the shower curtain holding a towel. I smiled, took the towel and let my hand stroke his as I did. Wrapping the towel around me, I pushed the shower curtain aside and found him standing there, naked, very awake, and looking at me with those damn eyes I have heard time looking away from. I let the towel fall into the wet tub as he held out his hand and helped me out of the shower, never taking his eyes from mine. Standing there in front of him, water dripping onto the floor, he slid his free hand down my right leg and between my thighs, pushing gently on the right one. I gave into his push and let my legs fall open as he slid his fingers in me. I gasped and let my head fall onto his chest, he kissed down my neck and to my breast as he stoked the inside of me with his fingers. My knees started to shake, but before I could fall, he scooped me up and carried me into my room, laid me gently on my bed and replaced his fingers with his mouth.

When we were finished, I laid in his arms with my head on his chest, eyes closed, I reveled in how good it felt to be next to him again, to smell him again, to feel him again. My eyes became hot and before I could stop them tears swelled and dumped out soaking his chest. I began to sob uncontrollably, startling him. He pulled me closer and kissed the top of my head. He never said a word. Perhaps he already knew, perhaps he was thinking and feeling the same way. He held me there, comforting me a little while longer, settling me just enough that I could collect myself together. Setting up in the bed I wiped my eyes and apologized for being a blubbering fool.

" I'm sorry, I don't know what came over me!"

Sam rolled over onto his side and propped himself up on his hand. He smiled at me and stroked my leg before speaking.

" Don't be sorry, you needed that, you needed to release that. Don't ever be sorry for needing to do that."

I took the hand that was on my leg and squeezed it, he brought it to his lips and kissed my knuckles. Smiling, I sniffed the last of my tears back, nodded and got out of bed. He watched me for a moment as I ran around my room naked, forgetting for a hot second what I needed to do today. I dug panties and a bra out of my drawers, rummaged through my closet for some jeans, settled for my old Navy Pt sweatshirt and Nike's.

" Um, are you going to get up and get dressed?" I asked Sam as I sat on the bed to put on my shoes. He chuckled, rolled his eyes and groaned as he rolled over onto his stomach. I stood, smiled a very mischievous smile, and smacked his naked ass, leaving a small red handprint on his left butt cheek. He yelled out and rolled over. I gave him my, *'don't make' l*ook. Throwing his hands up in surrender, he rolled to the opposite side of the bed and got up. Walking past me, guarding his behind, I smiled and shook my head as he walked backwards into the bathroom.

I heard the shower turn on as I went into the living room and gathered my notes and case files into a pile, grabbed a Tervis from the cabinet and poured coffee and creamer into it. I considered adding some bourbon and decided against it when my house phone rang. It startled me, almost causing me to drop the bottle of bourbon. I sat it down on the counter and answered the phone that was attached to the wall in the kitchen. I never disconnected the line, afraid that Amaria would call and it made sense when I moved to have a landline in the good old state of Oklahoma in case the power went out due to weather.

A scruffy, familiar voice comes on the line. " JJ?" Eli said

" Good morning little brother." I answered

He sighed and was silent for a moment or two.

" Eli, is everything ok?" I asked, concerned.

He cleared his throat and I could tell he was doing so to ward off any emotion he may have in his voice before he spoke. " Yes, everything is fine, I just wanted to hear your voice. How long are you staying?" he asked

I let that question linger. Unsure on the answer really. I hadn't thought about that.

" Um well, I don't know, I guess until this case is done, maybe longer." I answered, stammering over my words.

' Would you want to have dinner or maybe come by, Sarah would love to see you and you can meet the kids as well?' He asked

Smiling into the phone, tears clouded my eyes, realizing he just said *'kids'*. Last time I saw my brother was at his wedding to Sarah, four years ago. I don't even remember if I saw him at Amaria's funeral. I let the tears fall down my cheek and pool in the receiver. I swallowed hard, collected my voice before answering,' I would love that, Eli.' We set a date and I hung up the phone. I let the tears drip onto the counter. A light knocking caused me to wipe my face, turn and was greeted by Sam standing in the threshold of the kitchen looking at me curiously.

`` That was Eli, we made dinner plans before I went back to South Carolina." I told him as I grabbed my Tervis and retrieved a second to fill with coffee for Sam. Handing Sam his coffee, I walked into the living room and collected my notes and dug out Amaria's keys from the trinket box on the mantle. "Thank you baby girl, I promise I will not mess it up." I whispered as I took the keys. Turning around, Sam was closing his briefcase, slid his phone in his pocket and picked up his coffee from the coffee table he had placed it on. 'Ready?' I asked him, dangling the keys out in front of me. His eyes focused on my hand and keys dangling from it and he swallowed hard. He recognized the keyring and I could feel his heart skip a beat.

I gave a half smile and secured the keys in my palm and lowered my hand. I have to remember he lost her too. He had given her that key ring when she graduated high school. She had known him her whole life, I never had the heart to tell her he was her father, she loved him as Uncle Sam my partner and I didn't want anything to deter those feelings. I found her diary after her death, and quickly found out she already knew. "I'm sorry Sam, I"... I started to explain, but the look on his face told me I didn't need to for he knew what I was about to say. He walked over to me, placed his hand on the back of my neck and pushed his lips into my forehead.

" Let's go, we have a long day today.' He said as he took the keys from my hand, turned and walked towards my garage door. I unlocked the lock box next to the door that held the key. Each lock box has a different code. I had him install a double deadbolt on both garage doors so my summer tenants would not go into the garage. Tenants only had access to the door lockbox. Amaria's car was still parked in the same spot I left it, Eli had covered it with a drop cloth. By the looks of it, he had come by recently and started it. I had him come by once a week to do that very thing. I hit the garage door opener and let the sound of the door creaking open echo in through cemented walls.

The crisp cold air rushed in and as I retrieved my winter coat from the hooks on the wall next to the door. Pulling it close I stepped into the garage. Sam followed behind and walked around to the driver side of Amaria's car. I helped him to remove the drop cloth and expose Amaria's 1967 Ford Mustang. A car she spent countless hours with Eli and our father rebuilding and restoring to its magnificent glory. She was damn proud of herself, sitting behind the wheel for the first time as she fired it up and took it out for the first time.

We climbed in and Sam fired the engine up, my heart jumped as I felt the rumble of the car bring it to life. Sam looked over at me, gave me a smile and backed the car into the morning sunlight. The drive over to the Morris' was solemn and quiet. I watched out of the car window as we passed houses and cars, contemplating what I would say to Cassie's mom. We pulled into the circle driveway, through a rot iron gate, of a two story brick, colonial style house. Nestled back off the road a little ways. I felt an ice chunk dump hard from my throat into my gut and I swallowed hard. I tensed in my seat as Sam brought the car to a stop. He looked over at me and gave me a wink.

" Let's go!' he said as he turned the engine off and opened the car door. He walked over to my side of the car and opened it. Gesturing for me to get out. I took a deep breath in and slowly got out of the car. About that time the front door swung open and a very tired and aged man walked slowly out. A look of worry and confusion on his face. His reaction told me that he recognized me first. His curiosity shifted to anger, his stature went rigid and he folded his arms across his chest. Sam stepped aside, moving out of the way so I had direct line of sight of Andreas Morris, Cassie's father.

    I stood there and watched him walk slowly towards me and I braced for anything. I never took my eyes off of him. I didn't even notice Janice had walked out onto the porch. Andreas stopped about a foot from me, his eyes boring a hole the size of Texas in me. I shifted a little and shot a quick look at Sam.

" Detective Mallory." His voice boomed in my ears. I licked my lips and swallowed hard before I spoke.

" Mr. Morris, it's just Johanna now, I um, I retired some years back. I…" I looked over at Sam who gave me a nod of encouragement before I continued.' I have news on your daughter.' I let those words linger as Andreas blinked ferociously trying to comprehend what I just said. Janice slowly walked over and gently pushed Andreas to the side.

" What do you mean by news? Did you find her, is she ok?" Janice rambled. I blinked at the questions and looked over at Sam. I gathered myself and went into detective mode. I always hated doing death notices, it never gets easier. I swallowed hard, licked my lips before answering, " Yes we did, we found her body and we need you to…" Janice's wales echoed through the small valley they lived in, cutting off my words entirely. She collapsed into Andreas whose masculine stature was doing its best to not go down with his wife as he tried to hold her. Janice screamed and cried for what seemed like an eternity. Sam intervened at this point and helped Andreas usher Janice back into the house.

Andreas and Sam helped Janice to the couch and I sat across from her in a recliner. I positioned myself on the edge of it and leaned forward. My first instinct was to put my hand on her knee, but I held back. Unsure on how it would be received. Andreas had gone to the kitchen my guess is so Janice wouldn't see the breakdown that was evident on his face. I looked up at Sam and gave the unspoken signal to follow Andreas into the kitchen. He nodded once and followed Andreas. I rubbed my hands on the tops of my thighs, mainly drying the sweat that had accumulated on them.

I let Janice collect herself, as I found a box of tissues on the side table of the recliner and handed it to her. She shot me an angry, tear soaked look that softened as she took the tissues. She blew her nose and wiped her eyes. She fidgeted with the wet tissue in her hands before looking up at me. I met her gaze and gave her a slight nod of complete and utter understanding of how she was feeling in this moment. I think that realization is what prompted her to speak first.

" Johanna, I am sorry for how I treated you. I did not know, or maybe I did and was just blinded by my own grief to acknowledge what you were going through." She began

" Janice. No, please don't...' I started but she put her hand up to say 'let me finish'. I complied and let her.

" I have spent years angry at you that I couldn't see my own thorns in my eyes. But about two years ago I came across an old newspaper clipping about the execution of Marcus Orion and Amaria's name was the one name I recognized and in that moment it finally hit me and I cried. That same night I prayed, I prayed for forgiveness, for your forgiveness. I told myself if I ever saw you again I would tell you this very thing, and well, here we are. "

I gave her a kind look and placed my hand on her knee. She took it and gave it a squeeze. I nodded my understanding before I spoke, 'Janice, you have nothing to be sorry for, we both were going through a very terrible time. I spent years angry at myself for Cassie, for Amaria, for everything. I am so sorry we had to meet again under these circumstances.'

Janice looked at me with tear soaked eyes and squeezed my hand tighter. I asked her if she wanted to get ready to go see her daughter. She sniffed and nodded. Standing she held onto my hand and gave me a reassuring look. I watched her walk away, so poised and stoic, almost deliberately so. I noticed a picture on the wall she passed and I stood to go take a closer look, it was a photo of Janice holding a baby about eight months of age with huge brown curls and a chocolate ice cream covered face. So happy, so full of life. Sam cleared his throat behind and I turned to watch him walk into the living room followed by a very swollen eyed Andreas.

Janice emerged putting on her coat, she looked up at us all watching her, nodded as she zipped up her coat. Sam and I exchanged looks and walked towards the door. The Morris' followed behind in their car. Driving up to the Oklahoma County Coroner's office always has a foreboding overcast, a dark disparity of emptiness. Sam and I drove around to the back entrance, something we have done too many times to count, a muscle memory movement even in the car. Sam pulled the car in front of a door marked CORONER on it and turned the engine off. I sat silently watching out of the window at the door. Memories flooded my psyche and images of the last time I was at this very same door rushed through my mind, making my head spin enough I had to close my eyes to steady myself. Sam's head on my shoulder brought me around to my senses. I grabbed his hand without turning to look at him, I nodded and opened the car door.

I waved at Morris' car and walked over to them. I opened the door for Janice and she hesitated before slowly getting out of the car. She had the same look I did when I stood where she is now not that long ago. I reassured her that she could do this and stepped aside as Andreas came around the car and put his arm around her shoulders and ushered her towards the door. Sam was already at the door and rang the buzzer. The sound of heavy metal scraping as it opened echoed off the walls and shattered the silence of the morning. I nodded at Sam and I walked through the threshold first, the attendant let the door slam shut as Sam entered behind the Morris' causing everyone to jump at the sound. A sharp glare from myself and Sam made him lower his head and rush past us all to show us the way, disappearing behind a door marked EMPLOYEES ONLY.

Shaking my head, I assumed by that little fiasco, he was new,coming to a stop at a large picture window in the hall, a curtain hid what lay behind it, tucked away like some mysterious show waiting to be presented. The quiet was interrupted by Janice's sniffles and I turned to make sure she was ready. She was nestled against Andreas' chest, tears soaking his shirt and he nodded. I knocked three times on the glass and the curtain slowly shifted to one side revealing the cold gray of the room. A silhouette of a person was displayed on a stainless steel bed. The medical examiner stood ready at her head for my signal.

I turned once more to her parents and gestured for them to come forward. Janice's hesitation caused Andreas to gently pull her with him as he moved. Her shoulders were shaking and I saw the blood start to drain from her face. I signaled for Sam to stand behind them. Andreas positioned them to the left of me and nodded. I gave the medical examiner one swift nod and he ever so gently lifted the sheet off of her head and neatly folded it under her chin. Andreas watched intently, his grip on Janice seemed to tighten, trying desperately to either pull her into his chest or steady his own composure.

I watched his nostrils flare in and out hard, his jaw tightened. Probably remembering when he last saw his daughter. What she looked liked, what she felt like, what she smelled like, comparing every inch of this sleeping beauty he barely recognized. He asked to turn her head to the side. The M.E. complied, revealing a small strawberry shaped birthmark behind her right ear. This mountain of a man collapsed against the window, causing Janice to damn near be thrown to the floor. Sam caught Janice and the wall caught Andreas. I tapped again on the window signaling a positive i.d and to close the curtain.

Sam transferred Janice to me and I helped her sit on a bench behind us, as Sam rushed to Andreas and helped him slide to the floor. A ferocious roar escaped his lips, echoing the halls, rattling ear drums. Janice jumped up and rushed over to her husband and they sat side by side on the cold hard floor, sobbing. Sam walked over to me, sat next to me and placed his hands over mine. I hadn't noticed I was wrenching them. I nodded, regaining my composure and wiped the sweat from them on my jeans. Taking a deep breath I stood up and walked over the grieving parents. Kneeling, I helped Janice up and then Andreas came reluctantly, his knees wobbling some as he shifted back against the wall to steady himself. He sucked in air forcefully through his nose, closed his eyes and straightened his shoulders. Janice stood quietly next to me, her eyes fixed on the closed curtain of the window. I gently placed my hand on her shoulder, she slowly turned her head to me. Her eyes wanted to cry, but I knew the look of dried up tears.

Her heart was broken, but her soul was at ease at the same time. The worry, the wait, the suffering, now over. Conflicted between the feelings of happiness and sadness, unsure which she is supposed to feel. I gave her a nod of silent understanding in which she returned a sorrowful smile as if to say *'me too'*. Andreas, regaining his composure and stature took up next to his wife and she took her position again under his arm. Andreas stared at me, his look softened as his eyes met mine. The hatred eased and the hurt settled, relief settled in his brow, emptying out enough to allow grief to finally make her entrance and mourn his daughter properly. He nodded one swift nod at me and I returned the gesture.

Sam cleared his throat and ushered us all back down the hallway and out into the bright cold sunlight. The crisp air hitting before the warmth of the sun. I took a deep breath in to clear my nostril and lungs of the antiseptic sting that settled there. That stench, that sting, never gets a section in the *'used to it'* category of my brain. I informed the Morris' that they would have their daughter back in two days, and that they could prepare the necessary arrangements. I asked to be contacted once they had done that. Janice, still tucked safely in her husband's arms, wiggled out, walked over to me, stood in front of me a moment. I darted my eyes to Sam and back again to Janice. Janice cocked her head to one side, sheepishly smiled, and threw her arms around me.

I stumbled back a little, but steadied myself as I wrapped my arms around her in return. She squeezed me tight whispering *'thank you'* in my ear and kissed me cheek. Tears swelled in my eyes, burning them closed as they spewed out, soaking a small portion of Janice's hair. She let go and held my hands a moment before letting them drop and returning to her husband. He ushered her back to the car, helped her into the passenger seat, turned to me, nodded once more before returning to the driver side and leaving. I stood there a moment watching their car slowly drive away.

" You good Mallory?" Sam asked

I nodded and wiped my face before answering,' Let's go get this bitch." I held out my hand to take the keys from him. He looked at me curiously before dropping them into my opened palm. Sam called Lieutenant Hansen and informed him of the positive identification of Cassandra and the outcome of the meeting between the Morris' and I. We drove in silence after that to the station. I parked Amaria's car in my old spot, habit, muscle memory, who knows, but I did. I turned off the engine and stared out at the cruisers that were docked behind a chain link fence.

" You know you can't go with us when we serve the arrest warrant, right?' Sam asked

I shot him an angry confused look before answering," The fuck I can't! I am going to be the one that puts those cuffs on that crazed psychopath!" Sam laughed so loud that it reverberated off the windows. " I knew you were going to say that, but damn you should've seen the look on your face. Did you know that your nostrils shoot angry booger bullets when you get excited like that?"

Instinctively, I covered my nose and wiped, not getting anything on my hands, I punched him in the arm with the same hand, " Asshole!"

He continued to laugh at me, grabbing my hand and pulling me closer to him, kissing me. I protested out of fear of getting caught, before realizing I didn't have to do that anymore. I leaned into his kiss more and let his sweet lips take the pain I was feeling away just enough to not shoot angry booger bullets from my nostrils. " We have to go, Lieu is waiting for us." Sam said between kisses. I nodded, pulled back from him, punched him one more time and got out of the car before he could retaliate. He got out of the car and placed his hands on the roof, " You ok to go back in there?" He asked. I looked over at the building, took a deep breath in and started walking towards the door. " I guess so." I heard him say as he shut the door and fell into step behind me.

The department exploded in cheers of my name as old boys welcomed me and new ones sat confused on who or what I was. I have to admit it was damn good seeing them. I didn't realize how much I did until I was center stage of their embraces and curiosities. Same old boys and their same old shit. I giggled to myself and shuffled through them, meeting LIeu standing outside his office. " Your old desk still has your name on it." He said as I walked over to him. I looked back at it, shook my head and replied," Yes well, looks like you need the desk more than I do." Pointing back at the crowd behind me.

Agreeing, he asked,"Are you ready to finish this and go home?"
"Fuck yea." I answered as he handed me the arrest warrant.
" Who's coming with me?" I asked. Lieu pointed behind me.I turned to find the whole damn department standing waiting for my orders. Smiling, I looked over at Sam who had taken his position among the rest. He nodded at me as I raised the warrant above my head. I called out,' Let's roll' and the room erupted in cheers as they parted down the middle and let me walk out first leading my last charge.

We were prepared for anything, but luckily the arrest went without any major incident. The team had done a phenomenal job of surveillance and planning. I would like to say Julian came quietly but that was not the case. He resisted and tried to run out the back door, but that plan was futile, we had a secured parameter. Sam took him into custody and I watched from a squad car. He confessed to all the murders, but refused to answer anything about Cassie. I asked to be given a shot at him, met with utter resistance from the A.D.A, but with a little convincing from her boss, they allowed me to interrogate him.

His eyes went wide when he saw who walked through the door. Not a deer in the headlight look, more of a I know you look. Julie was about 7 when we arrested her dad, so the familiarity of me was there, but the comprehension of that knowledge had not settled. He watched me carefully as I walked over to the table, opened the file folder I had in my hands to display Cassie's body when she was found. I laid it in front of Julian and his eye twitched in recognition of the scene in the photo diverting his eyes to mine. The coldness evident behind the blank stare of them. A sinister combination to say the least. The birthmark shadowing the right one made the chilling glare of it slowly crawl down my spine.

I sat across from him and folded my hands in front of me. We sat there a moment like that, searching each other's eyes as if we would find the answers buried there. Julian sat back against the chair, the handcuffs clanking against the table as he deliberately slid them across it. He never took his eyes off of me. He reached up and took the file in his hands and tossed it back at me, sucking on his teeth at the same time. I stopped it from sliding onto the floor and repositioned it upside down in front of Julian again. Julian leaned forward, the chair sliding back some, the metal scraped the floor like nails on a chalkboard and my ears twitched against the sound. I stared back at him unmoved. He tried desperately to intimidate and although he was a splitting image of his father, he was in fact NOT his father. Marcus' eyes were cold, sullen, dead, Julian's eyes still held some vibrance and life of the little girl he used to be. I shifted in my seat and leaned back against the chair, folded my arms across my chest and gave my ultimate pissed mom look. Same look I used to give Amaria when she fucked up royally.

I saw a shift on Julian's face as he recognized the look. I imagine all mothers have 'the look' and every child, whether blood or not, recognizes that look. He became noticeably uneasy, his eyes shifted around the room like a loose ping pong ball. I stared even harder for a few more moments letting the energy I was giving off sink deeper into his soul, what very little he had of one. Sweat beaded on his head, his eyes glossed over and never stopped moving, his leg began to shake. Satisfied he was rattled just enough, I reached over and turned the file folder over to display Cassie's mutilated body, sliding it to the side to reveal an array of photos of bodies displayed in a similar fashion.

" You know, I thought I would go to the coast, get out of this black hole of a state, get some Vitamin Sea and live out the rest of my days not ever having to look again at shit like this." I said as I tapped Cassie's photo. Julian shifted in his seat. I leaned forward and picked up Cassie's photo and held it up at eye level. " I get all these other ones, Julie,' Julian's jaw tightened on his female name, ' I do, but why Cassie?" Noticing the shift in his stature I couldn't help but feel a sly smile curl from the right side of my mouth. Julian sat back against the chair and sucked his teeth.

" I mean I did do my research and I have to admit, I can't say that I wouldn't have lashed out against these bigots for their ultimate betrayal. I mean it must have been hard for you, being surrounded by all those women who thought that their femininity was more superior than yours. Not to mention their outright disdain for transgenders. I mean honestly I don't know what I would've done if I were in your shoes, Julie, I wouldn't." Julian's jaw tightened again and I could hear his teeth clenching hard against each other.

" But why Cassie, why hold on to her for so long, and then kill her?" I asked as I sat Cassie's picture down again in front of Julian. Shaking my head I leaned back and refolded my arms across my chest. " I mean did you know all along that your father kept her? Did he tell you where she was? Did you help him, Julie?" I watched Julian squirm in his chair, wringing his hands causing the cuffs to rattle from, jaw clenching tighter. He settled some and he tried so desperately to smile a cunning smile, but I saw the slight quiver in them as he did, as well as the shimmer of the beginning of tears. He swallowed hard to collect himself. I could almost hear his heart beat against his chest like drums in distant woods.

I sucked in a breath through my nose, leaned forward, rummaged through the file again until I came across an envelope. I held it up to Julian and watched his eyes flicker slightly to it and back to me. Again the desperation for intimidation struggling to be maintained. I toyed with the envelope for a moment, waving it slightly back and forth, holding it by my fingertips as if it were contaminated, before I sat back against my chair again, opened the envelope and held the photo it contained in front of me. I looked at it for a moment, staring at the sweetest image of a smiling baby and his mom, smiling even bigger, holding him up for the photographer to get the cutest picture. A knot swelled in my throat as I had a very similar picture of me and Amaria. I swallowed hard, composed myself and slowly turned the picture around, locking eyes on Julian's, watching the blood drain from his face as he recognized that sweet baby to be his very own. Julian's lips twitched slightly as he struggled to look at the photo. I slowly placed it on the table and slid it over to him. He looked up at me, licked his lips, straightened his back and casually turned over the picture. Curious on this notion, but knowing full well why he did it, I took the picture back and turned it over again only slightly out of reach from Julian.

" Why Cassie, Julie? This sweet baby in this picture does not need to grow and think his mother did these things. He does not need to have the same stain on him as you or your sister's did. He deserves to live a life of joy, happiness, not chaos and rage. Tell me why you did these things, tell me why you did what you did to Cassie. Tell me so I can help spare your life Julie."

" It's not Julie." Julian whispered through gritted teeth.

" I'm sorry? What was that?" I asked turning my ear to him as if I didn't hear him completely.

" Why Cassie, Julie?' I asked again, emphasizing his feminine name. He shifted more, his demeanor becoming even more agitated. " Did you have a nickname for your son Julie? I had a nickname for my daughter, and well Cassie's mom did as well. Her nickname was Squeaker, because she said when she started to crawl she was such a chubby baby that she scooted across the floor and she would make a squeaking noise on the hardwood floor. Did your dad give you the nickname Julie?"

His eyes shifted more, his jaw clenched more and his cheekbones looked like they would shoot out of his skin. He shifted his weight in the chair and fidgeted with the chain of the cuffs.

I leaned forward and tapped Cassie's picture, 'why did you do this to her, Julie?" I asked, tapping the picture annunciating each word with a tap.

" Why Julie? " I asked over and over again, tapping the picture each time. Julian, clearly pissed, started shaking his head, bringing his hands to ears in an effort to block my words. He screamed out and slammed his hands on the table and yelled, 'BECAUSE SHE WAS MY FIRST!" Stunned at what he had just said, I placed the picture back down, looking over at the two way mirror, I sat back against my chair. Broken, Julian placed his hands on the table and lowered his head. I sat there quietly, patiently waiting for him to explain.

Softly he began to explain,' She and I were friends in grade school, I thought she was so pretty, and I couldn't understand at that time what I was feeling or why. We weren't allowed to have company over. My mom, I guess she may have suspected what my father was, I don't know, but she never would allow anyone to spend the night, and if they came over, they were never allowed in the house. My father saw me walking home with Cassie one day, she lived three doors down from us at that time. He was outside working on his car when he spotted me coming up the street. I thought for once he was smiling at me, but he wasn't. He was smiling at Cassie…" His voice trailed off as he closed his eyes tightly to stave the tears from falling. Sniffing, he shifted upright in his chair and swallowed what emotions he had stuck in his throat before continuing.

" I have only seen him smile that way at my sisters, just before he would… have his special nights with them. I was so jealous of them then, not understanding what he was doing, just understanding the attention he was giving them and not I. He never touched me the way he did them, I got the belt mainly. He told me I was unclean for my impure thoughts. I guess he knew what I was before I did."

Julian looked down at his hands and fidgeted with his shirt. We sat in silence for a few minutes before he cleared his throat and said one final thing

" I will never forget what it felt like kissing Cassie for the first time, the lights from my father's camera burning bright illuminating our shadows on the walls. He left her there for me, you know. She was to be mine for all time."

With that he gave me a bone chilling smile and invoked his rights. The blood left my face, I could feel it pool just under my throat and squeeze. I slowly rose from the table, Julian never took his eyes off of me as I gathered up the file and photos on the table. I turned to leave, at the door he called my name and I turned to look back at him, terrified as to what would come out of his mouth. He cocked his head to one side, smiled again and said something that, thank goodness I did not have my gun on me, " Amaria was my favorite thing to do with him."

" You son of a bitch!" I turned to charge at him just as Sam opened the door and grabbed me from behind. Lifting me into the air as Julian began to laugh maniacally. Guards rushed in and secured him in handcuffs as Sam ushered me out of the room. I shrugged out of Sam's hold when my feet touched the ground and pushed at his chest. He stumbled back some but did not fold. He let me have my moment to grieve our daughter. I always knew that Marcus had help with Amaria but I couldn't prove it and he damn sure did not give anyone up. He took that information to the grave.

Sam was watching me intently and quietly. He just stood there so patient with a look of grief all on his own. My heart sank as I finally realized he had lost gravely as well. In that moment I realized how selfish and cruel I have been to him and I ached. I ached all over. I threw my arms around him and stretched up on my toes to kiss his neck and silently tell him I was sorry. He returned the hug and I felt his shoulders quiver as he began to sob silently in my arms. I held him there for a moment or two before he collected himself and let go of me. He smiled that million dollar smile at me, held out his hand to me and led me back down the hall and out of the building. We stepped out into the bitter cold of an Oklahoma winter, the sun neon bright but did not touch the sting on my face. I pulled my coat tight under my chin and shivered under it. I looked back at Sam and watched him step down from the sidewalk and stand beside me.

" Are you heading back tonight?' He asked me, looking straight ahead. I took a deep breath in, nodded, and took his hand in mine. I squeezed it and brought it to my lips before speaking, ' Not before I go see our daughter. You want to come?"

He looked at me and I saw his eyes were glossy from tears pooling in them, he nodded and said,' I try to go as often as I can." That statement stopped me on a dime and in that moment, I loved him even more. I felt all the anger, all the pain, leave my soul and sink to the ground, and I knew, I knew right then and there I never wanted to be without him again.

The trial was over before it even started. I followed it on the news and social media. Julian pleaded not guilty by reason of mental defect. He was found guilty but the judge sentenced him to a double life sentence in a maximum security mental institution with no chance of ever getting out. He felt that given Julian's history that was the best sentence possible for the good of the people. I called bullshit, but he will never leave the facility and the streets are safer. His sisters signed over any acknowledgement of him, basically disowning him and even filed a petition to have their last names changed and both are now living a life of relative ease on the west coast somewhere. Lieu retired and moved to Florida where he could be closer to his grandkids. He said he would trade shriveled balls for sweaty balls and that is exactly what he did. He calls me from time to time and once a year he comes to play golf in Myrtle Beach and we go to dinner . As for me, I came back the next day after Julian's arrest. I spent some time with Amaria and brushed the snow off her grave and took her her favorite flowers. Sam stood silently behind me, his eyes were closed and I did not interrupt his silent conversation with his daughter. We spent the night wrapped up together in my bed. I don't think I have ever slept so well. The next morning we had breakfast and he drove me to the airport. He kissed me passionately and told me he loved me. I sank into his arms and let him hold me a little longer. Three weeks went by before he called me. He asked me how I was and if I had a good new year. I told him I was doing ok, but it was a lie. Truth was, the Carolina cold alone was colder than any winter in Oklahoma the last three weeks. I wasn't sleeping and my bed went untouched since I had been home.

Talking to him, I heard a knock at the door. I told him I had to go and swallowed back tears as I put my phone on the counter. I checked my face in the mirror beside the door and wiped the tears from my face and straightened my hair before I opened the door. My heart leapt out of my chest when I saw that million dollar smile holding a cup holder with two cups of coffee and a brown paper sack between them. His bag sat lazily on the ground by his feet.

'Took you long enough.' was all he said, all I would let him get out before I threw my arms around him and kissed him, tears flowing. He nearly dropped the coffee. He sat it down on the small table I have on the porch and pulled me up into his arms and returned the kiss and tears.

Three years have gone by since that box was delivered to my office, three years since I first heard his voice, three years of blissful happiness. In those three years we got married and celebrated by the delivery of our second beautiful daughter. It was a difficult pregnancy and birth as being pregnant at 43 was not fun. But she came into this world fierce, screaming, and beautiful; with her daddy's million dollar smile and her sister's attitude. I still think about Julian from time to time. I have found myself sending letters and cards. Unsure as to why, they go unanswered and Sam swears I have lost my mind. But, for me I find it therapeutic. Sam helped me heal in ways I don't think I could have done on my own. I believe I have done the same for him. He smiles differently, looks at me with even more loving eyes, and that little girl is his entire world. I no longer feel the need to shiver when the cold comes calling.

GRIEF

Today I mourned for you
I let the tears flow and my heart break
I allowed myself to feel the pain you felt
I took all that away.
With each tear that dropped and each time I bowed my head to remember you
I took all that away.
This morning I listened to your screams and I didn't silence them
This morning I let you go free and didn't try to hold you back
This morning I gave you life and let you die
This morning I felt my heart break and mend back with gold.
This morning the little girl I buried to protect let go of my hand
This morning I mourned for you as I felt your bravery to let go.
This morning I healed her, through my tears and through my pain
I took it away.

TELL ME

She pulls me in close and whispers, "tell me."
"Tell you what?" I ask, " that you're beautiful, amazing, sexy ,loving and I'm so glad you're mine?"
She sighs, kisses me and whispers, "yes that, now tell me again."

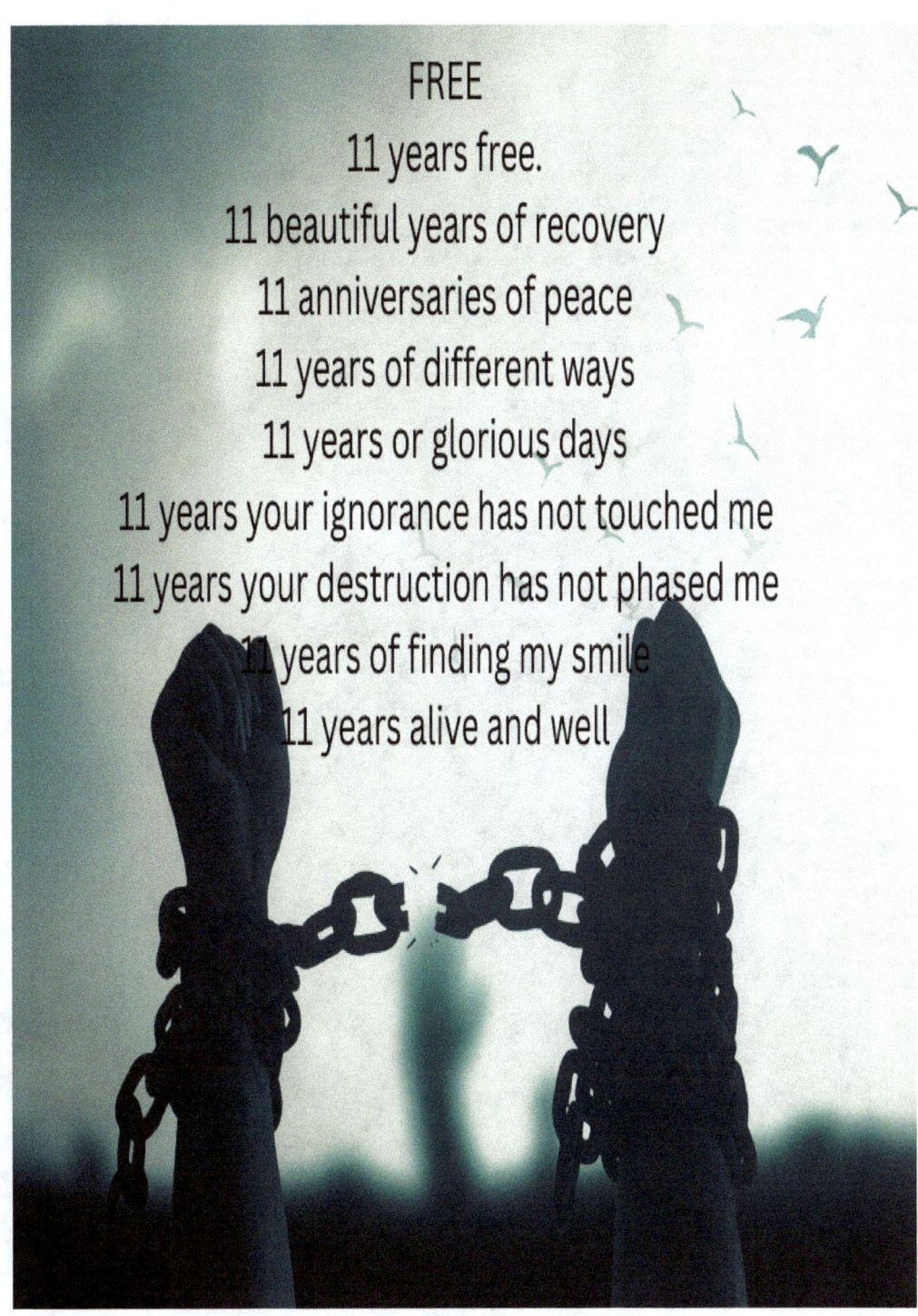

FREE

11 years free.
11 beautiful years of recovery
11 anniversaries of peace
11 years of different ways
11 years or glorious days
11 years your ignorance has not touched me
11 years your destruction has not phased me
11 years of finding my smile
11 years alive and well

I PRAY

I'll pray for you. I'll pray so that you won't have to,
I'll pray so that in hopes you'll get into the habit and pray for yourself and others.
I'll pray so that you will know it's ok to hurt, it's ok to be alone, it's ok to not be in control.
I'll pray for you to show you yes I care and no I don't have to always show it.
I'll pray for you so that your pain doesn't go without notice.
I'll pray for you so that in happy times you'll still rejoice the bad before it.
I'll pray for you in hopes that the vanity and the selfishness of you will fade away.
I'll pray for you because I know right now you won't pray for yourself.
I'll pray for you to share my strength, but I will not pray for you to be free, that is your choice to make.
I will not pray to make your life easier because that's a habit you must break.

BOUNDARIES

I will not apologize for how you feel
I will not acknowledge what you have deemed real
I will not accept your version of me
I refuse to see the way you see

Your interpretation of me is yours alone
I have dealt with my sins, I have atoned
I need no apology, I offer no explanation
The only acceptance is my own validation

ONE BULLET

Beautiful words delicately placed
on the dark side of grace
Gentle kisses on the wounds he made
Sweet surrender when you comply
Caressing the truth with a well placed lie

Singing a song of sweet release
Long sleepless nights praying for peace
Keeping his secrets under makeup
Covering mirrors afraid they'll speak up

Blinded by his sweet side
Shivering against the tide
Struggling against the waves
Screaming in my head counting the days

Finger on the trigger shaking in my hand
Praying for courage to take a stand
The ache in my heart stops me
Believing once again his phantom love for me

An endless cycle of catch and release
Not recognizing my voice when I speak
Small faces looking up at me
I have to escape, I need to leave

Same faces that he holds captive
Same faces that hold my will to live
As he tries to plant another seed
He smiles thinking he has me

Enough is enough
His reign is up
I steady my hand to take my aim
One bullet ends his game.

SWEET GIRL DIARY

Sweet girl let me talk to you
Let me help you find your words
Here you can say what you want
No judgement or scolding
No criticism, no hate
Just your words on paper
Flowing free and true
Sweet girl let me talk to you.

Sweet girl we meet again.
Come, sit, and take up your pen
Let it all flow from your mind
Let it fill the pages and flood the lines
Sweet girl , I'm so glad you're here
Take up a seat and let's talk a while
Your words are important and here they're cherished.
Doesn't matter what is written. Good or bad or in-between.
On these pages your voice can be seen.

Sweet girl, what's on your mind?
I see you're here again, do you need to unload, unwind?
Your words and thoughts are sacred
protected in these pages
Unburden your day and release your tension
You can even tell me what you forgot to mention.
Sweet girl, I'm so proud of you! Your words are beautiful just like you.
They don't have to make sense as long as they're true.
Keep writing sweet girl, even when these pages are done.

SIGHT

To the one who waits in my shadow, I see you
To the one who plots against me on the sidelines, I see you
To the one who falsely cheers me on, I see you
Just because I don't call you out, I still see you
The one who "praise my success" and choke on the very words, I see you
I see you in your full colors
I see you when you piggy back and slander backhanded comments
I see you when you don't sleep at night anxious of what I'll do next
I see you when you try to do things the way I do and fail
I see you
I do not have to say a word, I see you
I wish you nothing but the best, but I see you
I feel your eyes upon me as I walk away and exit you out of my life. Never again to allow your eyes upon me.
I see you.

RAGE

I sat with her in the cool dawn of light
I sat with her as she shivered with fright
I sat with her until her sobs quieted
I sat with her as fire sifted through her.
She doesn't know my name
She lets me hold her the same.
She holds onto me
She craves the fire I breathe
She lets go of my hand
When she finally understands
My name is Rage.

THE BEAUTY OF HER

I've often looked at this creature, this beautiful being in the mirror and didn't see beauty due to the darkness she was encased in. I felt the pain she had hidden behind her eyes, the lie behind every "I'm fine" and the tears that have soaked her pillow. I didn't realize then that I needed to see and feel all that in order to know what was needed in order to see the beauty of her.

TRAUMA
Crowded room
Empty halls
Deadly silence
Claims the walls
Eyes diverted
Minds perverted
Joy lost in the echoes
Stories unfold
Cold release
Walls built
a version of peace ?

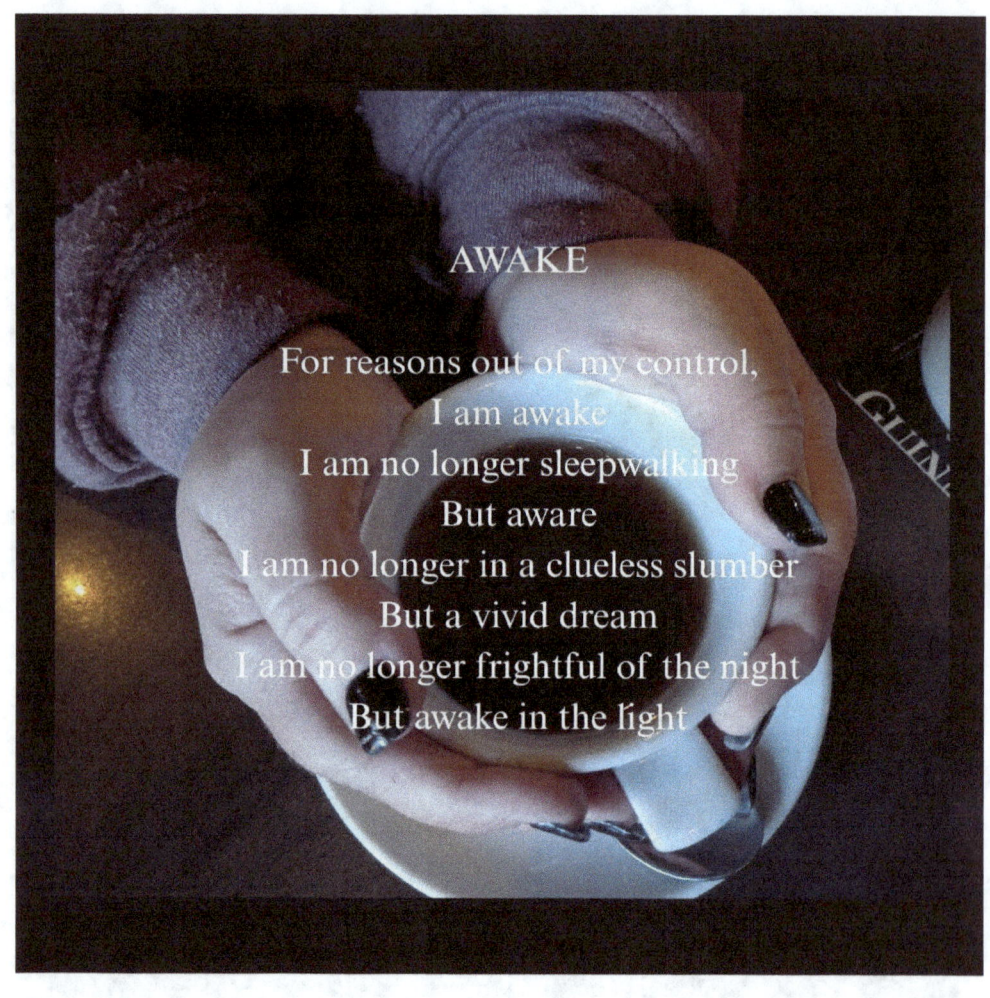

Time

As I sit here this morning and contemplate the night before. I am stricken by the notion of lost time. Gone, just like yesterday, gone to the last words spoken before I went to sleep. Stuck in the folds of my memory. '

Wondering how I let it all slip through my fingers with only small traces of sand left on them. Looking at the woman in the mirror and mourning for the girl she never was.

Listening to the voices playing in my head, searching for the one clock that ticks backwards. Longing for an hour glass to flip over.

Each moment a passage of fate that eludes the most conscientious. Each imprinted into the grey matter of oblivion. worried if time spent is time wasted.

It is the master of illusion, the ultimate escape artist and the greatest manipulator of all. Slowing to a point of insanity, speeding at the rate of exhaustion and yet moving at the same pace. Such a captivating beast and I find myself grieving and reveling in its magnitude.

Comforted by the belief that I have time, confronted by the realization I do not. Lying awake in the early dark of morning, struggling to slumber more. Listening to the quiet race against the clock.

Broken Mom

"No one ever talks about the broken side of being a mom, the nighttime cries and unheard sighs. The silent screams in the pantries, closets, and bathrooms.
The tears that stained the pillows, the sleepless nights, the worrying if she's good enough.
Contemplating giving it all up when her kids mistreat her simply because she is mom.
She's a broken mom, but she can handle it
She will pull herself together and carry on just like before.
She's a broken mom, but she will do it for them.
She's a broken mom, and knows one day they'll leave and she will wonder what the hell it was all for
She's a broken mom with anxiety so high it could run a football stadium.
When it seeps out sometimes and she loses her shit, she is deemed horrible instead of tired. Angry instead of worn out, abusive instead of fed up.
She's a broken mom and no one kisses her boo-boos, no one tucks her in at night, no one wipes away her tears.
She's a broken mom and still manages to get through the day. Sets her own wants and desires aside for the ones tugging at her shirt tail.
She's a broken mom and knows one day she will be left alone with it all, not realizing she already is.
She's a broken mom, and tells herself she would do it again in a heartbeat."

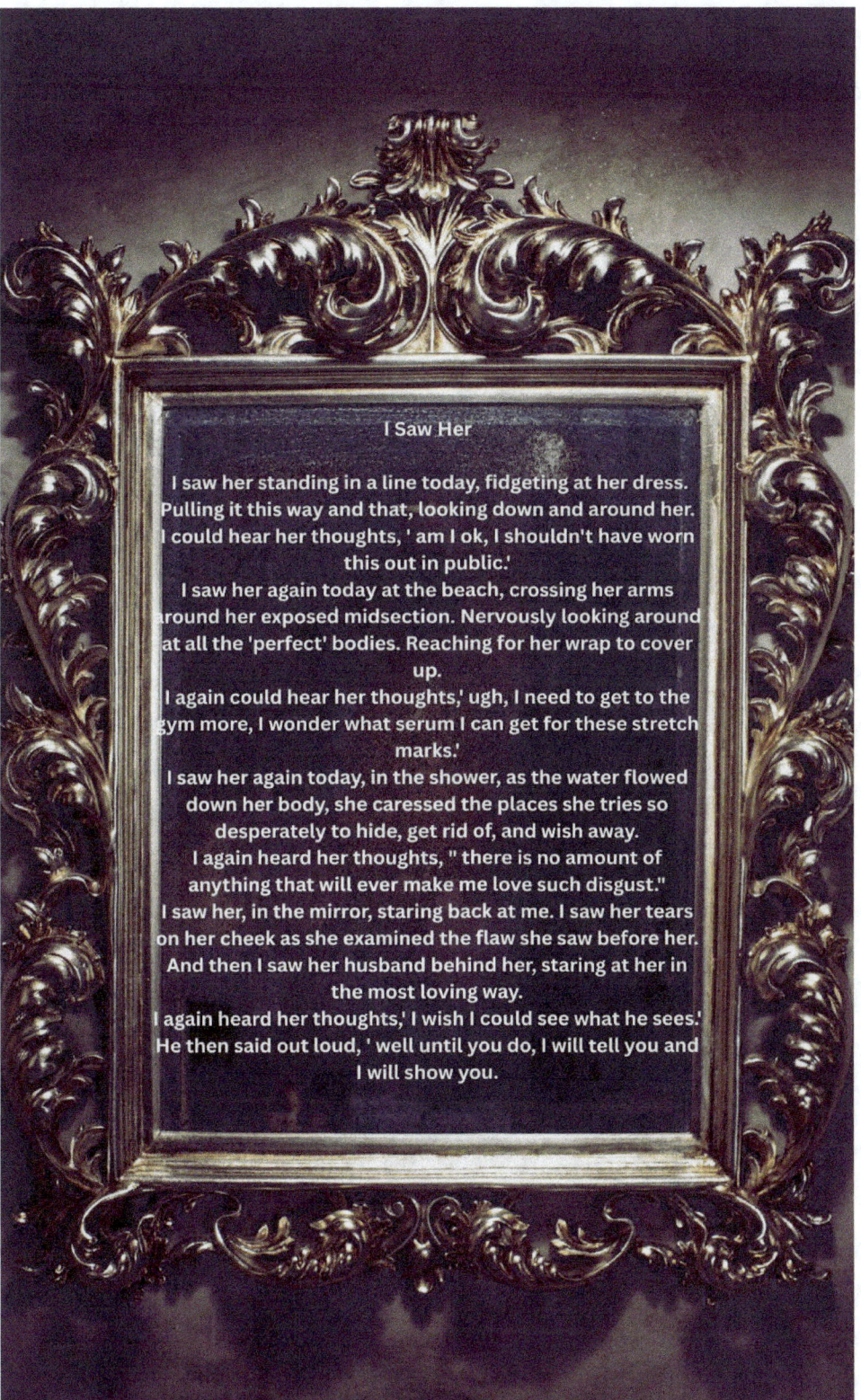

I Saw Her

I saw her standing in a line today, fidgeting at her dress. Pulling it this way and that, looking down and around her. I could hear her thoughts, ' am I ok, I shouldn't have worn this out in public.'

I saw her again today at the beach, crossing her arms around her exposed midsection. Nervously looking around at all the 'perfect' bodies. Reaching for her wrap to cover up.

I again could hear her thoughts,' ugh, I need to get to the gym more, I wonder what serum I can get for these stretch marks.'

I saw her again today, in the shower, as the water flowed down her body, she caressed the places she tries so desperately to hide, get rid of, and wish away.

I again heard her thoughts, " there is no amount of anything that will ever make me love such disgust."

I saw her, in the mirror, staring back at me. I saw her tears on her cheek as she examined the flaw she saw before her. And then I saw her husband behind her, staring at her in the most loving way.

I again heard her thoughts,' I wish I could see what he sees.' He then said out loud, ' well until you do, I will tell you and I will show you.

QUIET DARK.
Sitting in the quiet still of the dark part of the morning.
I am able to hear everything so clearly. Everything that is the loud of the light I struggle to keep quiet. The voices that scream in pain, the songs stuck on repeat, the cries from past lives.
Everything comes in one at time as I give the quiet dark permission to allow them to. Giving me the grace to listen to each and every one.
In the quiet dark
I can feel the arms of my ancestors cradling me, supporting the parts of me that hurt me the most. Whispering their words of comfort and wisdom. Taking away little by little, the sting of it all.
In the quiet dark
I can hear my guiding light giving me the strength to deal with the screams and cries, rejoicing hymns ring out as piece by piece the quiet dark of the morning claims another sliver of the chaos.
In the quiet dark of the morning is when I sense everything the most.
In the quiet dark

The Wake

I took a deep breath in, held it there, contemplating on whether or not I wanted to let it out. The sun has made its appearance and I slowly release the air trapped in my lungs. My eyes fixed on the ceiling and the dark quiet of the night slowly creeped away into the morning. I take another deep breath and close my eyes, begging for some sort of slumbered relief from the night's events. Anger exploded everywhere and no one slept at all. This house creaks and moans with every step and movement and the walls are paper thin at best. Cries and whispers seeping through the wallpaper and vents. Doors creaking open and people pacing. Nobody knows what to do when this type of feral anger explodes. When episodes of madness race through their heads. Going to our prospective rooms was deemed the right choice. Sort of an adult time out. I squinted against a beam of light escaping through a fold in the curtain and I turned to stare at it. Damn. I can still hear some rustling about, muffled shuffles from somewhere in the center of the house. I roll over to my side and slowly lift myself to sit on the edge of the bed. The wood floor was cold against my feet. My shoes were the only thing I took off. I looked down at my shirt and smoothed the wrinkles out and sighed heavily when I noticed the wine stain on it when he threw it at me. Fucker. I stood and began to unbutton it , letting it fall to the floor. I walked over to the door and turned the key sticking out of the door. Hesitated before I pulled it out and placed it on the table next to it. I stood there for a moment reminiscing on how many times I've done that very same thing for how many reasons. How many because of him. I ran my fingers down the wood, its rough texture sending a flood of sensations through me and memories danced at my fingertips. Shaking my head I turned away to walk to the bathroom when a slight knock stopped me. I half turned to look and wait and listen. Another knock and a soft voice called my name. I let out the breath I didn't realize I was holding. It's her. I called back to her and told her I was going to shower and that I would see her at breakfast. It was a moment before I heard the floorboards creak as she walked off. She was the only reason I came, the only reason I ever agreed to be a part of this charade. Damn her, I wished I didn't love her so much. The shower was cold, the hot water never seemed to reach upstairs in this old house, but I didn't mind. It gave me a well deserved shock. A refreshing electrical sensation to awaken my number senses, if only for a moment. I stood there longer than intention allows, letting the water run down and over me. I watched it pool around the drain before sinking into oblivion. Reaching for the soap , I tried to scrub the day and night before off, hoping the suds would somehow cleanse the hurt, wash the indecencies I,we, had partaken in last night. Damn him!

I stood for a while and let the hot water run over me and down my back, my head lowered staring at my feet. When the noise had settled to a dull roar in my head I turned off the shower and stepped out, the cold of the bathroom hit me and instant goosebumps sent a reminder to my bones that they don't like being cold. I had forgotten to turn on the wall heater, I forgot how old this house is and how not up to date it is as well. Wrapping myself in a towel I stepped out into the warmth of the bedroom, at least that has central heat and air. I stood in the doorway for a moment, scanning the room for my suitcase, finding it on the lounge chair in the corner, I made a beeline for it tripping on something in the process and went tumbling into the damn chair. " mother fucker! " I yelped as I regained my position and began searching for whatever damn goblin had tripped me. My eyes landed on the wine glass, the very same one that douche bag had thrown at me. SON OF A BITCH, I felt the heat rising as my ears started to burn and I angrily picked up the glass and tossed it on the bed. This is going to be a very long week, I thought as I donned my clothes. I contemplated drying my hair and decided against it. I never liked the ' blown out ' look and since yesterday's events were over, there was no need in looking fancy, at least not for today. The smell of coffee and bacon filled my nostrils as I opened the door. I took a deep breath in through my nose and let goodness flood into me. I smiled at who I knew was at the counter now kneading dough and humming gospels. I smiled and let my nose leave me downstairs. She sat at the table, legs swinging underneath, nose in a book and spoon dripping milk suspended in air as she slowly brought it to her mouth, pausing intermittently, before entering her mouth. I chuckled to myself, it must be a good book. She didn't even look up as I walked over and gave Frances a peck on the cheek and asked if the coffee was ready. "Chil', you done gave me a heart patter." She exclaimed, chuckling. I smiled at her as I reached for a cup above her head and poured a cup. " There's some real cream in the fridge if you don't want that imitation nonsense on the table." Frances said. " From your heifers ?" I asked. She gave me a sideways look and pursed her lips. I chuckled and kissed her again. Turning I met her eyes, I guess my voice brought her out her book. She watched me as I walked over to the fridge and poured some of Frances' sweet homemade cream into my cup." You drink coffee yet?" I asked her. She cocked her head to one side as a milk stained little crooked smile slowly emerged and I winked at her as I sat down at the table. She just smiled real big and I could feel the air from her legs as she exclaimed ,"NO WAY that stuff will stunt your growth and shrink your balls!" I damn near dropped my cup as I spit my coffee laughing so hard at what had just come out of that sweet girl's mouth! Frances wasn't having it, she turned quickly and threatened soap and no dessert for a week if anything like that ever came out of her mouth again, and the same went for me for encouraging her.

We looked at each other in the most mischievous way, both of us folded our lips in to try and contain the laughter. Frances stood there holding a wooden spoon out with one hand and the other on her hip shaking her head. " She should have been yours 'cause she a splittin' image ". She said and turned back to her biscuits she was making. I winked at her and nodded to her book. * What are we reading today?" I asked. She smiled and showed me to cover. "Moby Dick". "That's a big book for a small fry!" I said. She just smiled, shoved a spoon full of fruit loops in her mouth and went back to where she left off, but not before her eyes flickered up over my left shoulder indicating someone was behind me. She didn't need to do that, I had already smelled his cologne. He cleared his throat as he entered the kitchen. Frances already had his cup of coffee , just how he liked it, in hand and waiting for him. The newspaper neatly placed next to his bacon and eggs. Creature of habit is an understatement for his ways. She threw a look my way and I winked at her as Frances sat a plate in front of me. I thanked her and the three of us ate in silence. I stopped expecting any form of apology long ago from that arrogant bastard.

The others only trickled in when Frances yelled up the stairs to come get it before she threw it out to the hogs. All piling in and sitting silently around the table in their respective spots, all filled but one. One that sat empty, even though, out of muscle memory, Frances, sat a place for. She dare not take it away, not now.

I helped Frances clean the kitchen, not saying a word but I knew she wanted to. After she handed me the last plate to dry, she never used the dishwasher mama had daddy install for her to make it easier for her; she sniffed and I looked up from my wet plate. She slowly took it from me and placed it on the counter. Tears welling in her eyes rushed down her cheeks and her voice cracked as she started to speak. " Your mama…" she started as I shook my head and pulled her into me. I felt her body shake against mine as she cried. My own eyes burning with tears , not meant for my mom, but for her. I cried for her with her.

The events of the day after breakfast are a blur in my memory or memories. The day dragged on and the finality of the day was now upon us. I kept replaying the events of the night before. The ridiculousness of it, the embarrassment of it. It was stuck in my head on a loop making it impossible to yet again get any sleep.

The office was cramped and smelled of cheap cologne and cigars. My eyes wandered around the room scanning the dust crusted plaques and years old stuffed animals on the wall. I can't even remember how long this office had been in my memories of memories. The last time I sat in these chairs I was ten years old and I remember the cigar smoke hung in the air as it slowly burned out in the ashtray. My mother's eyes black from tears and Sir. Laramie Johnston III held a box of tissue out for her. At that time, being the youngest of four siblings and the last to be at home, I didn't completely understand; but I knew enough to know she had had enough. She wanted to get her affairs in order, she said as she held my hand and walked me into that office.

Sir Laramie talked a bunch of what was gibberish to me, that I now know was legalese, with my mother. Pointing to me from time to time and handing her paper after paper to sign. She did so, an occasional tear staining the signature.

I now stood in the very same room, holding onto the back of the very same chair, as Sir Laramie slowly walked into the room from his back door and motioned for me to sit. I cleared my throat and pulled the chair slightly away from the other and slowly perched myself on the edge.

" Sir Laramie, I am quite confused as to why you wanted to see me privately." I started

He cleared his throat and blew his nose into his handkerchief. He took a reluctant breath in and blew it out from his nose as he wrestled with a stack of papers.

" Well, Jennifer, I asked you here, because that is what was stipulated in your mother's will." he answered.

I shook my head, giving him a quizzical look, as I settled back into the chair. " I was not aware of any will."

" Of course you weren't, no one did. She knew, rathered, feared this day would come and wanted to be sure YOU were taken care of."

" I don't understand, why only me?"

He took off his glasses, took a clean tissue from the box on his desk, cleaned his glasses before responding. Almost like he was trying to see the answer through his lens like a crystal ball.

" As you are aware that you in fact have three older siblings, but what you're not aware of is that.." he trailed off as he held his glasses up examining them, looking again into the crystal ball of them. 'That YOU were the only child your mother ever had."

I damn near fell out of the chair at the revelation of that statement. I couldn't believe what I was hearing. I jumped up with my heart in my throat and my anger seeping through my veins. Sir Laramie was prepared for this reaction as he never made an attempt to settle me at all. He just let me pace around the room ,shaking my head , like a caged animal.

" What the hell are you telling me?' I damn near screamed at him

" Are you telling me that my brothers…." I began to hyperventilate and the room started to spin. Sir Laramie pushed a button on his phone but his voice was muffled and my vision blurred as I watched his assistant come rushing in to catch me as I fell.

I came to on the old leather couch that sat against the big picture window. The assistant had placed a small fan on the coffee table and angled it towards me. She was perched on a chair to the left of it holding a glass of water. A comforting and sympathetic smile placed gently on her face. " Oh you poor thing." she said as she handed me the water. I slowly sat up and swung my legs to the ground. I didn't quite trust that they would hold me just yet. I took the glass from her and slowly sipped the cool filtered water. It was refreshing as it cooled my still burning throat. She handed me some aspirin as Sir Laramie cleared his throat again.

" Jennifer, do you remember when you last saw me?' He asked

I nodded my head as I downed the aspirin.

" Vaguely" I responded.

He stood and moved to sit next to me on the couch. Holding a large manila envelope that had looked like it had seen better days. He held it in his lap for a moment, closed his eyes and handed it to me. He put his hand over mine as I started to open it.

"Just a minute, before you open that, I need to explain a few things." He said

I laid the envelope on my lap and sat back on the couch.

" I have been in your mama's family as their personal lawyer for as long as I can remember, but I knew your mama longer than that. My father was your grandfather's lawyer and closest friend and that meant that your mama and I knew each other on a more personal level. That affords me the liberty to tell you what I am about to tell you. My services and the services of this office, as my daughter will soon take my place, are now yours and yours alone. There was a deal made, long ago , between your grandfather and my father. To protect the Amerson family name. Which was your mother's maiden name."

He let that sink in, simply because he knew that I did not know her by that name. I looked, deer eyed at him and my breath quickened. I couldn't wrap my head around any of this. I didn't want to hear anymore, at the same time, I didn't stop him from speaking.

"The fortune, that is your daddy's ,is just that, and will in fact go to HIS sons. To be split between the three of them. You, being his only, legitimate , daughter, will get nothing unless one of your brothers agrees to give up part of their share. Your mother knew that would never happen. She knew, because she was not the boys' biological mother, she knew because their father made sure that they wouldn't. In his will, he stipulated that even though any brother may give up part of their share to you, that meant he would also forfeit his right to the remaining part to the other two brothers for them to decide whether or not to allow that brother to keep anything, if at all."

I felt sick to my stomach. I never wanted anything at all, I didn't care about money or any of that. I knew my father was a bastard, but this, this was worse. I took another sip of water and asked the assistant to switch for something stronger. She shot him a look and he nodded. She retrieved a bottle of top shelf scotch from the curio cabinet behind his desk and poured two.I took the tumbler glass she handed me and downed it in one setting. She had the second waiting hand out for me to take. I locked eyes with her as I slowly handed her the empty glass with one hand and took the one she held out for me with another. I took a sip and sat it down on the table.

" What about Allie, I asked?"

He looked at me a moment before he answered. "Allie? " he asked "We will get to her in a second."

He tapped the envelope that was still sitting in my lap." Let's open this together shall we" he said as he slowly slid from my lap.

He took out an old polaroid style photo. I could only see the back of it , but recognized the signature black glossy backing and the white striped bottom. He looked at a minute before handing it to me. I took it without looking at it. Not at first, I kept my eyes on his,searching for some sort of inclination or assurance. I saw only sorrow. I swallowed hard and looked down at the photo. My eyes scanned the glossy image as my mind tried to rationalize what I was looking at. I recognized my father right away, but the woman in the picture was not my mother. I focused only on her. She was smiling up at my father, holding a baby while another was clinging to her dress skirt. I recognized Jack, my eldest brother, as the little one at her feet. I dropped it as if it were on fire. My eyes began to burn as they swelled with tears. The assistant ,who had positioned herself at his desk, shot up and rushed the box of tissues to me. I assumed Sir Laramie had asked her to stay for my benefit.

" I know this is alot to take in, but we need to keep going." He pressed as he handed me the rest of the photos one by one. I watched a whole other life unfold before me in dingy photos. One after the other of my father and this mystery woman. It was the last one that finally gave my nerves the permission to be expelled from my stomach. The last one that set this whole thing on fire and everything came to a whole new light. The last photo he gave me was a newer one. It was of my father again, but older. Taken about 7 years ago, as another woman held in her arms a small baby wrapped in a tiny pink blanket. My mother stood to the left of my dad and Jack to the right of his wife.I knew who that baby was, that was Allie.I didn't understand at first until I noticed the arm around my brother's wife and how the smile on my dad's face was not of joy for his new granddaughter but of a coy smugness. I saw the unease on the face of my sister in law and I knew. I felt my face go hot and my mouth began to sweat and the mornings breakfast and scotch chaser came rushing back up.

The flood of memories came rushing full force back to me. The fights, the abuse, the torment, everything that went on in that house. I excused myself to the restroom and ran cold water over my face and rinsed the bile taste out of my mouth. I stood hunch over the sink with my eyes closed, trying to get a grip on what the hell was going on. A soft knock at the door came and the assistant's soft voice asked if I were ok. I told her to just give me one more minute. I looked up from the sink at the pitiful reflection that was me in the mirror and the storm clouds rolled into my eyes and the fire and anger I had when I left that prison I called home, returned. Pissed off and anger fueled I returned to the pair,who were talking and suddenly stopped as I walked in. Each staring at me as I made a beeline for the couch. I scooped up the photos that had fallen to the floor in my rush to the bathroom, took the remaining papers from Sir Laramie. I stood over him a moment before I took a step back. I politely thanked him and told him that the rest of the contents I needed some time and privacy. He understood.Before I left he gave me a warning. One I definitely listened to.

I drove back to my childhood home, fuming and determined to do whatever was needed. I didn't even notice Frances vacuuming the floor as I stormed past her, up the stairs I ran, skipping every other step. I didn't notice she was right behind me. I flew open my bedroom door and made my way to the chair my luggage was on. My clothes were still strewn about the floor.I didn't care. I shoved them back into my luggage and slammed it shut. I was gathering my toiletries when Frances' voice startled me out of my rage fueled mind.

" Jesus Franny, what the hell are you doing?!' I yelled at her

She did not respond, but reached up and slapped me across the face.

" I raised you better than that chile'!" She scolded.

I snapped out of my tantrum and rubbed the stinging on my cheek. I apologized as tears poured out my eyes.

She tsk'd and held her arms out for me and I all but fell into them. " Hush now." she said. " Everything is going to be alright.' She rocked me a moment and let me cry ugly on her. As she has done so many times before. She pushed out at arms length, wiped my face and kissed my cheek. She reached into her apron pocket and pulled out an envelope.

"Come, sit with me a minute baby, Mama Franny has something for you." She took my hand and led me to the bed. She went over and shut and locked the door and put her finger up to her lip to shush the room. She sat next to me, positioned herself to look at me and took my hands.

"What you hold is for you and you alone. Your mama gave that to me the day she died. Her last words to me were for me to promise to only give it to you after you saw Sir Laramie. And by the looks of it, that is where you have been today."

I looked down at the crumpled envelope, I could tell it had been folded and refolded several times. I began to open it and Frances stopped me. " Oh no my sweet girl, not here. Not ever here. Take your leave now girl and take her with you."She warned

" Allie?"

" I can't just take her. " I said

She tapped the envelope and said" Yes you can.'

She stood and retrieved a small red suitcase from beside the vanity. I hadn't noticed it before, Frances must have brought it when she followed me.

She stood there a minute holding the suitcase in front of her before she spoke.

" She gets out of school in two hours. I told her you would pick her up and that you were going on an adventure. I called the school and let them know you were going to pick her up early so she is expecting you. Go get her, leave this place and never look back. Everything you've discovered today will make sense in the coming days."

With that she held out the suitcase, tears were already streaming down her face. I slowly walked over to her, took the suitcase and hugged her tightly. I knew I would never see her again.

" Where are we going Aunty Jenjen?" she asked

" On an adventure my sweet girl." I responded

" Are we ever coming back?" She asked

"No" I answered

" Good" she answered as she looked out of the window and began humming her favorite little tune.

My mother was not a fool. She spent a lifetime with a man who thought she was. When I was ten years old she was diagnosed with breast cancer and she knew then that she could not allow another daughter to be his.

The boys' mom was never identified, they never knew anyone else besides my mother. Although, I think Jack may have suspected. He was always distant and short with my mother. But she loved him anyway. She loved fiercely and in the end that love sought its retribution ten fold. My mother knew that Allie belonged to my father. Her mother confided in my mother that she was forced upon on her wedding night. She told my brother, who is a splitting image of my father in every way, beat her for allowing it. She was beaten and bribed until she couldn't take it anymore and filed for a divorce. A divorce handled by none other than Sir Laramie. Three days after the divorce and she was awarded full custody, she was killed in a car accident. No one thought it was just an accident. But the coroner ruled it that way. My brother assumed that he was the sole custodian of her, but what he didn't know was he was wrong, he was dead wrong. She knew, just like my mother knew when I was 10, she could not let another daughter be theirs. In the documents I now possess told a story,one that destroyed the very name I no longer recognize as my own. That sweet girl and I are now and will forever be, Amersons. As far as my father and brothers? Well, the IRS took care of that so-called fortune, and my father died destitute. Leaving his boys the same.

Final Thoughts

My reflection is capable of starting a revolution in my soul."

- Oprah Winfrey

"I remember when I heard these words, I remember the state of mind I was in when they were presented to me. I had done something I never thought I would or could do. I joined a pageant. Not just any pageant, not your typical, have to be a size 2 and look great in a swimsuit pageant; but one that forced me out of my comfort zone, forced me to face the demon that had latched on to me since birth it seemed. The one that every time I looked in the mirror, I saw a fat, disgusting, ugly force of nature. One that only fed on those words. One that my entire existence told me I would never be "beauty". That would never be a word anyone would ever describe me. That pageant changed all that for me. It hurt like hell through this shift. Some of the battle wounds are still a little tender. I still remember the pain it took for me to face that mirror demon and realize it was all a lie. Having a complete and utter breakdown(true story) in a Dillard's dressing room trying on dresses. Something I had no idea what or even how to do. No one to consult, save a few photo exchanges with my person. Crying I sat on the bench in the dressing room, half naked, staring at this ... person in the mirror and something told me to just breathe Rachael, and I took several deep breaths in and out, fished my headphones out of my purse (I carried them everywhere at that time) and the very first thing I heard was ,"My reflection is capable of starting a revolution in my soul." Tears stained my cheek as I looked up at that very reflection again and in that moment, I thanked her for everything. Thanked her for her softness, her curves, her ability to carry life, her fortitude to still be here."

www.ingramcontent.com/pod-product-compliance
Lightning Source LLC
Chambersburg PA
CBHW050329010526
44119CB00050B/730